EFFORTLESS RVING

HOW TO BUY THE PERFECT RV, SAVE MONEY CAMPING, AND OVERCOME ALL MAINTENANCE CHALLENGES BEGINNERS FACE.

J. W. WARREN

TABLE OF CONTENTS

Introduction   v

1. What Type of RV Should You Buy   1
2. How to Buy your Rig   27
3. RV Towing   47
4. Planning your First Trip   57
5. Getting your RV Ready for the Voyage   77
6. RV Internet   87
7. RV Preventative Maintenance   102
8. The RV electrical System   129

Conclusion   147
About the Author   149

INTRODUCTION

J.W. Warren

Hello, my name is James Warren, and I am 21 years old. 21 years old? What could I ever learn from A 21-year-old? Don't you have to be "old" to RV"? Well, times are changing and changing fast.

When I was 8, my parents bought a class A Forest River RV, and told my siblings and I that we were doing home school. A few months later my parents proceeded to sell our house, and the journey began. As I matured, I realized I wanted to turn this into a lifestyle one day. That day came way faster than expected. At the age of 17, I started a successful online business.

The business ended up taking off, and by the end of senior year, I had decided to pursue it full-time. I realized I could do anything I wanted. My parents bought a new RV, and I took over Bertha (aka our old RV). I was 18, alive and free. I wanted to be in control of my own life, and RVing let me do that. RVing gives me the same freedom running my own business does. I can do whatever I want, whenever I want.

Two kinds of people exist in this world....

Those who follow their dreams and those who live an unful-filling life, just trying to get by. It's the American Dream to live the life you desire, be free, and control your destiny. Set your-self free from a boring 9-5 and a controlling boss, and build a life you love. Many people are stuck in the corporate rat race, the ordinary, vicious cycle of boring office life. A few people enjoy it, but for most, it is pure misery.

Many people fear the change and discomfort that comes with chasing their dreams. They will complain about the monotony of their lives but never want to take the great leap into the unknown. Les Brown's famous quote sums it up well, *"for a lot of people, a known hell is better than an unknown paradise."* The differ-ence between people who follow their dreams and those who don't is simple. People who follow their dreams make the deci-sion and take action on it. This decision doesn't have to be a huge one. But it can be, lol. I decided I wanted to live life on my terms, and I went out and did it. Your dreams are the things that make you think, *"Well, that would be kind of cool."* They could be things you mention randomly and offhandedly. With courage, you can turn that small inkling into a cosmic empire.

Now I am not telling you to drop everything and become a full-time RVer. However, if you desire to start RVing and travel the world, GO FOR IT, even if it's part-time. The world needs more dreamers. Look into history; almost all successful individuals were vivid dreamers. It would be very hard, dear friend, to look at yourself in the mirror and convince yourself that you have achieved your dream if you live life conforming to other people's terms and ideas.

Your success should be defined using your terms, and those terms don't need others' approval.

Most people thought I was crazy when I decided to forgo college at the age of 18. I didn't care. Nothing was going to stop me from living out my dream.

Since I started RVing, I have never felt more freedom. The RV lifestyle sure isn't easy, but I wouldn't have it any other way. I get to spend my time doing whatever I want. Hell, I had enough time to write my own book. I love RVing, and I can see why it's growing so fast.

RVing is on the rise, with contributions raising $114 billion in the U.S. economy in 2019 alone. This was a 15% rise from the previous year. It seems like RVs have found their way back into the hearts of the American population.

This lifestyle has many benefits:

• flexible schedules

• freedom to work from anywhere in the world

• spending more time with loved ones

• and much, much more

I believe with my whole heart that life is more fulfilling when you pursue your dreams and passions. An RV lifestyle gives you the freedom to live life on your terms. You will be your boss, creating your rules and experiencing adventure once more, just like when you were younger. You can wake up whenever you want or go to sleep as late as you wish. You can experience the peace of building a small fire in the open or reading your favorite book under the glare of beautiful stars.

As a beginner in RVing, the learning curve is steep, and many RVers quit before getting over the hump. This book will teach you the things beginners need to learn before venturing into the

RV world. With proper knowledge, RV travel is much easier than most people think.

In this step-by-step, nuts-and-bolts guide to kicking off your RV dream, you will learn:

• How to Buy an RV the right way

• How to save money on the road

• How to do RV maintenance

• How to get internet and Wi-Fi

• What you need to pack.

• The ins and outs of an RV's electrical system

• Road safety tips

• Let's dive right in....

WHAT TYPE OF RV SHOULD YOU BUY

I t's true; your maiden voyage will certainly be the most exciting and undoubtedly the most nerve-wracking. But while RVing may seem like a tall order for most amateurs, it doesn't have to be intimidating. All you need is a willingness to learn and a sense of adventure.

When I started the RV lifestyle, I didn't realize how versatile RVs are and how many classifications there are. I struggled to grasp all the different concepts and terminology used in RVing. You're probably in the same boat, especially if you are a beginner. But don't fret. The slight learning curve of an RV lifestyle shouldn't be too overwhelming. In this chapter, you will learn the different variations of RVs and what to expect from each of them. The term RVing describes a wide range of camping experiences, most of which have a minimal resemblance, so let's start from the very, very top. I would typically recommend a midsized motorhome with minimal driving skills and more feature comforts for beginners.

But, I must also admit that choosing the right kind of RV is a personal choice dependent on variables such as:

- How many people are traveling with you?
- Will you use the RV frequently?
- What's your budget?
- Will you be going on extended trips or short trips?
- What features are you looking for?
- The list is endless!

This chapter explores the basic features of recreational vehicles to help you narrow down your search.

There are three main types of RVs.

- Motorhomes
- Towable Trailers
- Campers

Motorhomes

You've probably seen these bus-like RVs in the movies. Motorhomes are designed with the same framing and artist's impression of mercenary buses and trucks. What does this mean for your adventure across the world? Lots of extra space to get comfortable, move around, and stretch. These units are part vehicle, part house, so they don't need towing. They get classified as either A, B, or C according to their sizes.

I. Class A motorhomes

Class As are your classic motorhomes. They are the longest, largest, and heaviest RV option available on the market today. They are the most lavish RVs, and with that comes high costs. Class A motorhomes have state-of-the-art amenities and furnishings such as ample closets, luxe leather sofas, luxury kitchen appliances such as microwaves, ovens, and refrigerators. You may even find bathtubs and washing machines in some of them.

They are perfect for full-time RVing, extended trips, family traveling, and people who want to live luxurious on the road. Class A motorhomes are designed with an enormous panorama windshield and high seats, making them great for country viewing as you drive along. They are built on the chassis (a load-bearing framework that supports an object) of either commercial trucks, vehicles, or buses.

Features of Class A motorhomes

- Average Length: 21-45 feet
- Average height:11-14 feet
- Price range: 90k-500k
- They have 2 AC units
- They run on 50 AMP (AMPs are the base unit of electrical current)

Pros

- Lots of living and storage space
- Can handle the most amenities
- It can comfortably accommodate 4-8 people
- Great driving visibility
- It has bigger fuel tanks and water tanks
- High towing capacity

Cons

- Low mobility
- Very expensive
- Low fuel economy, on average, they only get 7-13 miles per gallon

Class A motorhomes run on both gas and diesel

a). Class A gas motorhomes

Class A gas motorhomes are cheaper and easier to service when compared to diesel motorhomes. Gas engines offer more acceleration, and their performance is excellent in high altitudes and colder climates. Beware, with the engine in the front, gas motorhomes can be a little noisy while traveling.

Gas motorhomes are the perfect fit for occasional travelers because you will save a lot on upfront costs. Also, Stick to gas motorhomes if you plan on staying in cold climates.

b). Class A diesel pushers motorhomes

Diesel pushers are the definitive example of RV luxury. They offer more modern residential-grade and high-quality features when compared to gas motorhomes. The main difference between Class A diesel and Class A gas motorhomes is the price. Depending on the type, diesel pushers can have an additional cost of anywhere between $50,000 - $100,000. Diesel pushers offer more torque power, little to no noise and smoother rides compared to their gas counterparts. They are built on a motor-vehicle chassis with the diesel engine located at the rear end. These engines are perfect for cross-country adventures and extended trips. Many RVers prefer diesel pushers for full-time travel. Not only is the diesel engine durable, but it also lasts longer than gas engines. For this reason, diesel pushers are pretty expensive.

I recommend Class As for full-time RVers because they are fully furnished homes. The big living area, extra amenities, and extensive storage will benefit you greatly. These RVs are great for those who want to have a more comfortable and luxurious experience while out on the road.

II. Class C Motorhomes

Class C Motorhomes are the typical family-friendly motorhome that doesn't break the bank. They are also known as mini-motorhomes, but they provide the luxuries of sizeable RVs in a cheaper, scaled-down version. They are built on a tracked chassis and can be either gas or diesel-powered. Ford, Mercedes Benz, and Chevy are some well-known manufacturers of Class C engines. They are easy to recognize because they come with an exclusive loft over the cab that contains either a bed or storage space. They are the most diverse out of the motorhomes and can vary quite drastically in their designs.

Class Cs can be compact, full-size, or super-sized, with compact Cs being the most popular. They come with either a Mercedes cutaway chassis or Ford Transit. The big-daddy of this group is the Super-C which uses a Freightliner or Ford F550. You will enjoy luxury home amenities such as roomy kitchens, large living spaces with plush leather seats, small dining room tables, queen-sized or fold-out beds, and private bathrooms. They can comfortably accommodate 4-6, but you can squeeze up to 8 people with a bit of creativity. They may not have all the luxury features of Class A motorhomes. Still, most people are usually comfortable with the options provided by Class C motorhomes.

Class Cs are usually easier to drive than Class A motorhomes. They are excellent towing machines, giving you plenty of flexibility when you are out on the road. They look like nothing else in the market; for this reason, Class Cs are very easy to pick out.

Because Class C Motorhomes run on 30 AMP power, they have more electric options during travel. Most RV parks are short of 50AMPs (I will go into the details of RV electrical in Chapter 6). With a shorter chassis, Class C Motorhomes can fit into more campsites than the larger Class A. This makes them much more flexible when compared to their class A counterpart.

Features of Class C motorhomes

- Average Length 22-35 feet
- Average height 10-12 feet
- Price range 70k-200k
- It runs on 30 AMP
- Has one AC unit

Pros

- Smaller and more mobile than the Class A
- Easy to drive (compared to most RVs)
- Can handle lots of amenities
- It can comfortably accommodate 4-6

Cons

- Not near as much space and storage as class A
- High Price
- Low fuel economy

Class Cs usually run anywhere from 8-15 miles per gallon, making them slightly more fuel-efficient than Class A motorhomes. Multiple Class C floorplans are available. This makes Class Cs great for weekend campers and part-time campers that want to get away with their families. They may not be as expensive as Class A Motorhomes. Still, the initial cost of Class C Motorhomes is very high compared to other models such as campers and trailers.

Class Cs are big and spacious, but they can be dim in the presence of other RVs such as Class A motorhomes or travel trailers. If you are interested in luxury camping, you may want to find alternative RVs that offer more options.

III. Class B Motorhomes

Class B motorhomes are fuel-efficient, small, agile, and ready to hit the ground running. The living space they offer is ideally suited for smaller groups. Picture them as Class C's little sister.

Every square inch of these sleek, modern design motorhomes packs lots of amenities in the compact space. They are also known as camper vans or B-Vans. Class B motorhomes are built on a van chassis and resemble large vans rather than a "houses on wheels." Class B motorhomes are limited to a certain degree. They can accommodate far fewer passengers than either Class A or Class C motorhomes. However, Class B motorhomes can go almost anywhere, just like standard vehicles. Class B Motorhomes are very flexible; and can make a smooth transition from a camping vehicle to an everyday city ride. They can and will often take up no more than a single parking space. You can easily store your Class B RV in places like your driveway or a big garage. Class Bs provide a flexible travel schedule because there are few places they can't go.

On average Class B motorhomes, you'll find features such as a Murphy bed/couch, small kitchen and dinette, bathroom or wet bath, and an awning. The Murphy bed or fold-out sofa provides you with extra space while you're not using it. Also, note Class B kitchens are usually tiny. It is rare to find luxuries such as ovens, microwaves, and countertop kitchen space.

Due to lack of space, most Class Bs have one wet bath. A wet bath is a shower, bathroom, and sink combined (sounds fun). Most Class B's come with an automatic awning that helps you stay cool by protecting you from the sun. The awning allows you to extend your living space to the outdoors, creating more room at the campsite.

The features of a Class B motorhome do not compare to either Class A or C's; however, higher-end class B motorhomes have many of the same luxuries and amenities.

Class Bs are lighter and have a better fuel economy than other motorhomes on the road. They can cover anywhere from 15-25 miles per gallon.

Features of Class B Motorhomes

- Average length: 15-25 feet
- Average height: 9-10 feet
- Price range: 50-175k
- Runs on 30 AMP

Pros

- Small and easier to maneuver
- Easier to store
- Better gas mileage
- It can comfortably accommodate 2-4
- Less pricey when compared to other motorhome options

Cons

- Expensive (for their size)
- Limited space and storage
- Few Amenities
- Limited floor plan
- Smaller holding tanks

Class B motorhomes are ideally suited for solo travelers or outgoing couples who love adventure. They are also great for people who enjoy the minimalist lifestyle and are willing to pack up and travel wherever they want. Just be prepared to let go of a few comforts.

. . .

RV Trailers

Travel Trailers

Travel trailers are super-popular. This is your basic pull behind that uses a standard ball and coupler hitch. These rigs are also known as "bumper-pulls." That's because when they first gained popularity in the 50s, they would be attached to a tow car's bumper. Of course, this has changed. Modern travel trailers are secured to the tow vehicle's frame using a hitch.

They are the most widely sold and most varied type of towable RV. Travel trailers come in many forms, from simple models with chuckwagon kitchens and jelly-bean fashioned structures to fancy ones with sliding doors and picture windows. This rig is also versatile in weight; you can choose from an ultra-lite rig to a heavier half a ton version. No doubt you've seen one at a campsite or being pulled down the highway by a pickup truck.

Travel trailers are often cheaper than motorhomes and fifth-wheel trailers (which I will cover after this). With the low overhead clearance, travel trailers can fit perfectly into many places fifth-wheel trailers and Class A motorhomes wouldn't.

Inside, you will find all comforts of a residential home. Like all non-motorized RVs, travel trailers have no driving area, which gives RV designers room to take advantage of a wider variety of available floor plans. The unlimited number of travel trailer variations and types makes this trailer ideal for many campers. Depending on the trailer's layout, expect to find features such as large dining rooms, residential kitchens, separate bedrooms, full-size bathrooms, showers, and more.

Travel trailers are typically not as luxurious as the fifth-wheel trailer or Class A motorhomes, even with their great amenities. Most travel trailer owners use a portable generator located outside the vehicle or nothing at all. Beware that the portable generator can be very noisy.

Due to their versatility, many travel trailers often have bunk beds and separate bedrooms to accommodate large families. A travel trailer's weight fluctuates and can vary anywhere from 4,000 lbs to 10,000 lbs. Travel trailers have varying mileage depending on the tow vehicle's capacity and the size of the trailer.

As an owner of a travel trailer, always know the towing capacity of the vehicle. Don't be deceived; a travel trailer takes just as much if not more skill to maneuver and drive than other towables. It is highly challenging to tow a travel trailer because of where the hitch point is. The turning radius isn't excellent either. Strong winds can easily throw you around. Fortunately, you can easily drop your travel trailer off and move along with your tow vehicle as you please. Most importantly, make sure you can back up the trailer before hitting the road. Backing up a travel trailer is very difficult and takes lot and lots of practice.

Most states will not allow you to carry passengers in the trailer when traveling. So in most cases, you can only bring as many people as your car allows. This means you and your family will be crammed in your car all day as opposed to a motorhome on travel days. Please make sure to check the state laws on traveling with passengers in the trailer before you hit the road.

Features of Travel Trailers

- Average Length 12-35 feet
- Average height 10-12 feet
- Price range 10-100k

Pros

- Low cost
- Can quickly drop off the trailer
- Very versatile
- It can comfortably accommodate 1-8 people
- The travel trailer can work for many different types of RVers

Cons

- Need to have a large truck or SUV to tow a travel trailer
- Difficult to maneuver and backup
- You cannot travel inside of trailer (in most states)

The travel trailer is an excellent fit for people looking to get away on the weekend with their families. I also recommend this rig to full-time RVers who don't want to spend a fortune on a big motorhome. Travel trailers are also great for boondockers;

with travel trailers, you can get way off-grid, especially with the smaller travel trailers.

Travel trailers provide campers with the freedom of having a complete living unit while out on the road and a vehicle that lets them enjoy their travels.

Fifth Wheel trailers

Yes, a fifth-wheel can imply something other than that single, unnecessary person always tagging along on dates. Among outdoor enthusiasts, it alludes to a type of rig that provides adventure lovers with the same benefits as that of bigger models without the stress of moving around with a full-blown house. The U-shaped coupling mounted above the tow truck's cargo bed led to its reference as a "fifth-wheel."

Fifth-wheel trailers are the largest towable RV on the market. Instead of the conventional hitch ball system found on travel trailers, fifth-wheel trailers use a fifth-wheel hitch to tow. The fifth-wheel hitch can only work when attached to the bed of a pickup truck. A fifth-wheel's tow hitch centers the RV's weight, making it very stable and easy to tow compared to travel trailers. Owners of fifth-wheel's often detach the trailer from their truck, allowing them to go where the trailer cannot.

The slide-outs and extended lengths make fifth wheels one of the most spacious RVs. Some fifth wheels have floor plans with up to six slide-outs.

The fifth wheel is quite an upgrade from the travel trailer and is great for people who do not want to commit to a motorhome. Fifth wheels are typically more luxurious than travel trailers. With fifth-wheels, you can get the nicest amenities for the best price. A typical fifth wheel will include a residential kitchen, dinette, island, large living area, couches, a bedroom, and a full-size bathroom.

The fifth wheel gas mileage varies, but it is not very efficient. If your truck runs on diesel, the gas can be very costly, especially as you tow bigger fifth-wheels.

Features of fifth-wheel trailers

- Average length 25-40 feet
- Average height 12-13.5 feet
- Price range 40k-150k
- It is designed with two AC units

Pros

- Plenty of living space and storage space
- It has lots of amenities and luxuries
- Variety of floor plans and layouts
- Easier to tow (compared to travel trailer)
- It can comfortably accommodate 4-8people

Cons

- High price
- You cannot legally travel inside the trailer
- Bad fuel economy
- Due to their large sizes, fifth-wheels may not fit into all campsites
- Fifth-wheels are not nearly as versatile compared to the travel trailer
- Unhinging and backing up can be a real challenge

The fifth wheel is great for RVers who stay at campgrounds for an extended time and people who like to live a lavish and spacious lifestyle. A fifth wheel is also a great solution if you already own a pickup truck capable of towing it.

Like any other type of RV, it is vital to ensure that the towing vehicle is strong enough to handle the weight of the RV and all the camping gear inside of it.

Hybrid Trailers

Hybrid trailers are a blend of travel trailers and pop-up campers. If you have been looking for a lightweight, small RV with a decent amount of space, look no further than the hybrid trailer. These trailers have pop-outs in addition to traditional slide-outs. Both the pop-out and slide-outs provide additional living space. The interior of hybrid trailers is similar to that of conventional travel trailers, except the pop-outs on the sides are made of canvas. You can expect a dinette, bathroom, shower, stove, and a fridge. Larger rigs may even have couches in the living area. Hybrid trailers also have excellent bed spaces. The beds fold out of the camper's sides, opening up the floor area for other people to sleep.

Features of hybrid trailers

- Average length: 13-15 feet
- Average weight: 3,000-7000 lbs
- Price range: $15,000 -$40,000

Pros

- It can be easily towed around with either small trucks or SUVs
- It can easily fit in most campsite locations
- They have more space than meets the eye

Cons

- The fabric walls are thin, and nights can get noisy
- They are expensive for their size
- The fabric sides don't offer protection from harsh weather conditions

RV Campers

Truck campers

Looking for a tow anything, go anywhere and camp anywhere type of rig? Look no further than truck campers. Forget fifth-wheels and Class As. If you want ultimate freedom and adventure, you want a truck camper. Truck campers are designed to glide into a pickup truck's bed and automatically turn the pickup truck into a motorized recreational vehicle.

They can be mounted and demounted from trucks very easily. These campers are called demountable campers in Europe and tray campers in Australia. Truck campers are pretty small, and 42 states don't even recognize them as RVs. They don't take up much space and will only occupy two parking spaces at most. They are versatile and can fit anywhere, from driveways at a friend's house, sandy beaches, unpaved logging roads, and standard parking lots. You are basically able to go everywhere a pickup truck can.

Just like the trailers in many states, it is illegal to ride in the camper while driving so you can enjoy your travel days crammed in your truck. Make sure to check the laws for each state because they vary when it comes to traveling in truck campers. You can expect to get 10-15 mpg, but gas mileage varies depending on the size.

Features of Truck Campers

- Average floor-length: 8-12 feet
- Average height: 10-12 feet
- Price 10-100k
- Most come with rooftop air conditioners

Pros

- Easy to maneuver
- Can go almost anywhere
- Easy to boondock
- Can comfortably accommodate 2-4 people
- A truck camper has great depreciation value

Cons

- Limited space and storage
- Have to have a truck
- Difficult to load and unload truck
- Over time, the camping trips will take a toll on the truck
- Not all trucks can house truck campers

The truck camper is great for solo RVers and couples who want to boondock off-grid and visit more remote locations. As long as you do not mind the limited space, a truck camper should work just fine.

Pop up Campers

While so many choices exist in the rabbit hole of RV options, many RVers prefer lightweight, more affordable pop-up campers. They have ultralight maneuverability, smooth-riding axles, and extra space for all your treasured belongings. In simple terms, a pop-up camper is an RV that can be collapsed down into a large box on a trailer. They slump into light trailers for transportation and pop up during camping.

Pop-ups look like small trailers or fancy tents at the campground and are short and flat when collapsed. Not only do pop-up campers cost significantly less compared to other options, but they are also cheaper to maintain. They are easy to tow because of their lightweight nature and can be towed by most modern cars.

Pop-up campers can go just about anywhere, which makes them perfect for boondocking and over-landing. Their compact nature makes them easy to haul through more rugged terrain, and their size adds to the ease of fitting them into tight spaces.

Pop-ups fold down into a smaller size allowing for easy storage and travel. This rig is family-friendly, and many families choose this option over other RVs because they are very affordable.

With pop-up campers, you can expect two queen-sized beds, a small kitchen sink, stove, a small dinette (that folds into a bed), and built-in storage. They have a hard base extension with canvas sides that provide extra sleeping space. Many are surprised to learn that some pop-up campers have air conditioning. Some also have rooftop units, window-mounted units, and portable AC units. Even when popped, space and amenities are limited compared to larger RVs.

Gas mileage depends on your vehicle, but on average, expect to lose around 7 mpg while towing a pop-up camper. Thankfully the aerodynamic structure saves gas mileage significantly.

These campers have very thin walls, so loud noises will easily penetrate and cause disturbances. If your generator is running, the noise will be on full blast all night. If you are sensitive to noise, a pop-up camper may not be the best fit for you.

Pop-ups can be susceptible to harsh weather, especially the smaller models. Storms and winds can cause severe damage if you are out camping in a pop-up. I would recommend checking the weather before setting up a pop-up camp.

Features of a Pop-up camper

- Length: 8-16 feet (packed) 16-30 feet (popped)
- Height: 8-12 feet (popped)
- Price Range: 5-40k

Pros

- Low price
- Compact and lightweight
- Great mobility
- Easy to store
- It can comfortably accommodate 2-4 people

Cons

- Few amenities
- Can be noisy
- Fragile
- Having air conditioning is certainly not a guarantee
- Setting up and breaking down your pop-up camper can be very time-consuming

Pop-up campers are a great and inexpensive choice for solos or small families that want to get away and experience nature for a weekend. This rig is also great for those who want to test out the RV life without total commitment.

Teardrop Campers

Teardrop trailers are small, towable RVs. They are bold, striking, and easily recognizable due to their distinct shape – round on one end and tapered on the other. They are shaped like teardrops, hints, the name.

Teardrop campers are the cheapest trailer option available on the market today. The simplest ones are nothing more than a bedroom on wheels. The clever design and vintage look of teardrop campers make them a favorite among many campers. Many RVers customize their teardrops with retro paint, exciting color schemes, wooden exteriors, or a simple color to match the tow vehicle.

With a teardrop camper, you can enjoy the outdoors without having to worry about generators, electronics holding tanks, and all the amenities that come with large RVs. One huge benefit of teardrop campers is that they can be towed by most cars, so you can take this rig virtually anywhere you want. You don't even need vehicle storage facilities. It's very easy to fit your teardrop in the driveway or squeeze it into the garage.

In a teardrop, you can expect a galley, queen-sized bed, and storage units. A teardrop galley is an outdoor kitchen consisting of cabinets, cooking space, and some kind of cooking device. Like the pop-up, many teardrop campers do not come with an AC unit; however, many install their own later on.

Teardrops can get pretty cramped because there isn't enough space to accommodate people standing up. The limited storage and space compartments limit the amount of gear you can bring. Most teardrops lack fully equipped bathrooms, so you will need to get creative to take a shower. Hygiene facilities at the campground and national parks will definitely come in handy when you are out on a teardrop trailer.

Features of teardrop campers

- Length: 8-13 feet
- Height: less than 6 feet
- Price: 5-20k

Pros

- Price
- Mobile
- Light weight

Cons

- Lack of space
- Few Amenities
- No indoor kitchen
- No bathroom

The teardrop is a great trailer for newbies or people who are just learning to tow and maneuver a trailer. It works for those who don't want to spend a fortune and be free from the worries of large recreational vehicles. As long as you adore nature, you'll love this rig.

2

HOW TO BUY YOUR RIG

W elcome to the not-so-secret club of prospective first-time RV buyers. This club has been dominated by retired outdoorsy travelers who prefer the tranquil and serenity of nature rather than some drunkenness on a Caribbean cruise. These days, times are slowly but surely changing. Even young Americans (like myself) are now looking for exciting ways to get out and experience nature on their own time.

Have you joined this bandwagon already? Do you want to make your first RV purchase? Well, not so fast!

There's a lot you need to know before you pull out your checkbook. What do most people do when they purchase an RV? They go to a dealer, look at a few rigs and end up buying the one the salesman recommends. Contrary to popular belief, RV salesmen are not always on your side. That's why you must be educated and know what you want.

There is more to buying an RV than the simple act of making a purchase. This kind of investment is enormous, long-term, and exhilarating. Purchasing an RV is exciting, but it doesn't always work out, especially for those who haven't educated themselves with the right kind of information. This chapter goes over the whole process of buying an RV to help you understand the nitty-gritty and the bigger picture in the RV buying process. You will also learn to make sure your RV doesn't come crashing down on the way home.

Floor Plans

A floor plan is an estimated drawing that shows the rooms and structures (or an RV in this case) from a birds-eye-view. Floor plans help design the furniture layout, electrical wiring systems, and much more. While floor plans differ from one manufacturer to another, many of them follow several basic patterns. Manufacturers create floor plans with many unique features and designs. Some floor plans prioritize entertainment and living space, while others focus on sleeping space and storage.

Whether you are looking for the most space or coolest layout, always make sure your floor plan is flexible. Versatile floor plans are very beneficial when selling your RV later on. For example, it would be ideal for you or a future buyer to transform a bedroom into an office.

A good floor plan usually has an excellent room transition; for instance, the flow from the living space to the outside area should feel natural. If you work from home, make sure your office gets enough light and is in a quiet location.

Your main priority with floor plans should be to make sure everyone who lives there has a place to sleep. This is an obvious one; however, you would be surprised how many people overlook this.

RV Floor Plans You Should Know

- **Rear Storage and Living**

REAR STORAGE AND LIVING

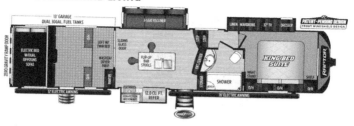

Photo credit: keystonerv.com

This floor plan is unique. It features a combined rear garage/living area to give you plenty of options. The garage creates enough room for packing things like a few bikes, a kayak, an ATV, or a motorbike. This unit's sleeping space is ample because of the available rear compartment, making this plan perfect for families, couples, or friends.

- **Minimalist**

THE MINIMALIST

Photo credit: winnebago.com

If you are looking for lots of storage space, mobile chassis, and bare-bones accessories, look no further than a minimalist floor plan. Minimalist floor plans are usually found in pop-up campers and Class B motorhomes.

They are ideally suited for boondocking in secluded areas. You will enjoy extra storage space, a minimal kitchen, and a compact living area. A minimalist floor plan works well for RVers who live an adventurous life outside the RV and just need enough space for sleeping and cooking on the inside.

- **Chef's Delight**

A CHEF'S DELIGHT

Photo credit: entegracoach.com

If you appreciate culinary arts and enjoy a warm homemade meal, the chef's delight floor plan is for you. The chef's delight floor plans come with ample kitchen space, storage space, and office space to delight the culinary RVer. You will find this type of layout on Class A, fifth wheel, and Class C RVs. Key features of this floor plan include a residential refrigerator, full-sized microwave, overhead cabinets, and lots of countertop space.

- **Entertainment-Focused, Front-Living Plan**

FRONT-LIVING, ENTERTAINMENT-FOCUSED FLOOR PLAN

Photo credit: fleetwoodrv.com

Are you a movie fanatic? A sports lover? Or do you enjoy watching TV? Look no further than the Entertainment living plan. This plan is commonly found in large rigs such as the Class A motorhome. The open-concept floor plan has a front-living that's perfectly suited for a large number of people. Distinct features of these plans include large sofas, chairs, several TVs, and a decent-sized kitchen. If you're into tailgating, you will fall in love with the large awning and outdoor grill.

- **Rear Bunkhouse Family Floor Plan**

THE ULTIMATE REAR-BUNKHOUSE FAMILY FLOOR PLAN

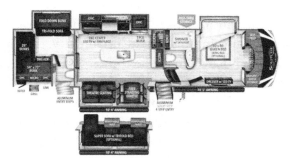

Photo credit: granddesignrv.com

Are you done sharing bathrooms? Do you want extra sleeping space for the kids? Then take a look at the Rear Bunkhouse plan. This floor plan is perfectly designed for families that need space. Enough storage and living space is a necessity for RVing families of all sizes. Families should gravitate towards this floor plan because it provides multiple compartments, outdoor facilities, several different sleeping arrangements, and entertainment space. This plan also offers bunk beds which provide extra storage and living space.

These are just 5 of the most common floor plans. Visit an RV dealer or local RV shows to get a good idea of the floor plan that meets your needs. You can also check RV manufacturer's websites and YouTube videos to get a good feel for different floor plans.

- **Height**

Many people prioritize the maneuverability of an RV and over-look the height. I am here to tell you that your day can go from great to horrible in a matter of seconds if you overlook the importance of knowing the height of your RV. The height of your rig is something you must be conscious and aware of at all times. Depending on its height, your rig may not fit under every overpass and bridge. Entering some parking lots or drive-throughs will be very hard if your RV is too tall. Ignoring the height may have disastrous consequences for your RV's roof.

Not to scare you, but after a fatal underpass accident in Durham, NC, an entire website was dedicated to the victims. A quick scroll through the site reveals some horrible scenes of the accident. One look and you will understand why you don't want to be a low clearance bridge or underpass victim. Your RV comes with an owner's manual, which lists the dimensions of the rig, including the height. The height listed in the manual may not be inclusive of the appliances and additions to your RV.

If something like an AC rack is on the RV roof, you need to know its height. I recommend physically measuring the addi-tional appliance with a tape measure. Physically measuring will give you the most accurate results and peace of mind knowing the exact height of the RV.

The Federal Highway Administration has no regulations set for recreational vehicles, but every state has its requirements. For example, both commercial and recreational vehicles in Georgia shouldn't exceed 13.5 feet. If you have a tall class A motorhome, you need to be careful and know each state's rules. A general rule of thumb is that Eastern states are typically more strict on height limitations. Western U.S states are a little more flexible. For example, Nebraska and Colorado allow a height of 14.5 feet for commercial and recreational vehicles. Alaska is the most lenient, with a maximum vehicle height of 15 feet. You should familiarize yourself with height regulations in states you plan to visit.

Apps

Two apps I recommend to help avoid disaster on the road include:

- **COPILOT GPS**

This is an app specifically designed for RVs. All you need to do is input information about your rig, and CoPilot will find an appropriate route for your weight and height. It costs $29.99 a year, but it will keep you and your rig safe from dangerous roads. I recommend this app if you have a very large and tall RV.

- **In route**

This app allows you to devise a path based on various options, including curviness and elevation. Travelers heading out to mountainous regions will especially appreciate this. This app costs $39.99 a year, and I only recommend it if you plan on traveling the mountains often.

Buying Process

As the old saying goes, *"The two happiest days in an RV owner's life: the day you buy the RV and the day you sell the RV."* Buying your first RV is a process that requires time, effort, and extensive research. It is an exciting investment, but you must arm yourself with the proper knowledge.

The process can be a little daunting, especially for novice buyers. But you can develop a plan to minimize headaches and avoid unnecessary stress down the road. Take some time to outline the specific features you want, financial options, payments methods, and negotiation tactics. Springing for a brand new, fully-loaded RV could be a real temptation, but don't get in over your head. Before you pull the trigger on an RV, I recommend doing some planning and spending a little time in a rental RV.

Before you ever walk into a show or see a dealer, you need to do your research and should know;

- The right price for your desired model
- The financing options available
- Whats the highest price you're willing to pay?
- How much discount are people getting?
- What's the dealer's reputation?
- What's your credit score?
- What's the depreciation rate of the RV?

Read online reviews about things like the brand, manufacturer, and dealer. The more information you are armed with, the easier the whole buying process will be. Always try and stick to a cash purchase if it is a viable option. Avoiding unsecured personal loans will save you a fortune in the long run. They usually carry high interest rates.

Buying New

The debate of Old vs. New is as old as time. Should you buy a new RV or an old one? The opinions on each side of the aisle are solid and different for multiple reasons. Your preferences and financial situation should be the ultimate determinant. Each side of the argument has its pros and cons. Buying a new

RV is like buying a new car; it smells good, everything looks nice, it's clean, and it comes with a warranty.

When buying new, local dealers and shows are the first places you should look at. Sites such as rvmiles.com and gorving.com list the most significant RV shows in the United States and Canada. You can visit the sites to find and compare all types of RVs. While attending these events, always be patient and conduct a price check before giving over any money. New RVs are extremely overpriced most of the time, so knowing your facts and how to negotiate can save you thousands of dollars.

The RV dealer will often try to get you to focus less on the final sales price and more on a lower monthly payment. NEVER FALL FOR THIS. MONTHLY PAYMENTS DON'T MATTER. If you want to pay monthly, that is fine; however, the price is the same. The salesman will try to throw you off by offering you free things like an inspection or free seasonal campground passes. Discount them and tell them you are sticking to the price.

One of the main benefits of buying a new RV is that they come with a warranty. An RV warranty basically covers repairs and expenses that come up. Buying new takes the stress out of having to find a good warranty (which can be quite the process). RVs always have high maintenance and service costs, so you'll benefit from warranty coverage (I will discuss insurance and warranties later).

It's worth knowing that many new RVs come with their own set of problems and "bugs" straight from the manufacturer. You'd be surprised to learn that a used RV is often in slightly better condition than a brand-new RV.

Manufacturers often ship RVs to dealers without doing a final inspection. And even when the inspections are complete, the dealers are expected to fix whatever the manufacturers missed before selling the RV. Some don't do this; others do. For example, water damage is a common problem in new RVs. Many go unchecked for sealant leaks as they sit in the dealership. To avoid water duds, always check the RVs interior well before making a purchase. Buy a moisture meter (on Amazon) and check the interiors. Anything that registers over 20% is wet and should not be bought. Moisture meters are around 50 dollars, but in the end, it might save you from buying a dud.

You can only negotiate for the best deal if you are knowledgeable enough. So please do the research; you'll save hundreds, if not thousands.

Advantages of buying new

- Buying new is fun and exciting
- It comes with a warranty
- There are no past damages
- Buying new is safer and has less risk

Disadvantages of buying new

- High price
- High insurance premiums
- Many times New RVs are not in as good a shape as used RVs

Buying used

Should you buy used? For me, there is no contest - go for used. Heed my warning because this is a cautionary tale about the mistakes you shouldn't make. The thought of buying used can be a little scary for newbies. What if you inherit a complete mess? What if you are unfamiliar with all the repairs needed?

Well, don't let fear drive your decision. I have talked to so many people who drive used RVs. I have never met a single experienced RVer who recommends buying a new coach. The more you understand RVs, the more likely you are to lean towards buying used. Buying new is fun, sexy, and exciting; however, I always recommend that newbies buy used. On average, an RV loses at least 25 percent of its value the minute you drive it off the lot, so buying an RV that's a few years old can save you a fortune. If you are willing to do your research and take some small risks, you can find great deals. It's possible to buy an RV at half of what it costs when it is new, and it will still look like a new ride with all the bugs fixed.

One of the most common places to find great used rigs is rvtrader.com which filters results based on what you are looking for.

Some other common places to buy a used RV include;

- Craigslist
- eBay
- Facebook Marketplace

In many cases, used models are often better-equipped than new ones because the prior owner may have completed upgrades and added new perks.

Like buying new, you want to make sure you go into the purchasing process knowing what a good deal is and what is overpriced. Always see if you can access maintenance records from the previous owner because this will give you confidence in the RV.

When buying used, it is essential to check for things like water damage and rust because they can be a pain to deal with down the road. Whether buying used or new, you should always get a

3rd party inspection. Sometimes previous owners try and hide things that inexperienced buyers won't be able to pick up on.

After inspecting the RV, I recommend asking the owner to take it for a test drive. Don't buy the rig if the owner doesn't let you take it out (major red flag).If the seller is committed, they may even offer to pay for that inspection but don't buy the RV if the seller is not willing to have it assessed. A downside is that used RVs don't usually come with an automatic warranty. Depending on who you buy it from, you may need to buy a warranty package (I go over warranties later in the chapter).

Advantages of buying used

- You will save a lot of money
- You may get an RV you love that is no longer in production
- Used RVs have cheaper insurance rates
- RV is broken in and will often have fewer maintenance problems

Disadvantages of buying used

- It can be risky
- It does not come with a warranty
- Not as exciting as buying new

Inspections

The RV lifestyle is a dream-fulfilling goal, and falling into an emotional trap is quite easy. This dream come true can turn into regret in a matter of seconds if you overlook inspections. Many first-time RVers don't have the experienced eye, and the last thing you want to do is dip into essential savings for repairs. What if you are a vintage enthusiast who just made their purchase of a 1963 Dodge Travco (Class A motorhomes that were first produced in masses), and you want to bring it back to its former glory? Wouldn't an RV inspection be apparent? One of the most critical parts of the RV buying process is a thorough inspection before purchasing the vehicle. Professional inspections cost anywhere from $150-1,200. The price varies depending on the type and size of the rig.

You may spend a few hundred dollars on professional inspection now, but you will be saving yourself from buying an RV with multiple problems and issues that may not be noticeable at first glance.

When looking for an independent RV inspector, don't limit your search to their certification. You should prioritize experience; look for RV inspectors who have many inspections under their belt.

Finding a well-qualified inspector takes some research, but the peace of mind that comes with knowing you made a good purchase is worth it. A good inspection ensures that you haven't missed any detrimental problems before investing thousands of dollars.

I always recommend getting a professional inspection, as long as you can find a well-experienced inspector.

What does the inspection consist of?

Ask the inspector if it's okay to walk with them during the process. However, some inspectors may prefer working alone so that they can concentrate fully. If they accept, you will learn a lot.

The inspector should check all the major parts such as the paint condition, if the doors and the windows work, if the electrical system is functioning, if the tires are in good shape, and etc. They should document things such as the condition of fabric and décor. Some inspectors will even take photographs. When you are purchasing a high-end unit, make sure the engine coolant and transmission get inspected. Also, check that the VIN (vehicle identification number) matches the title and ownership.

All these factors influence an RV's value.

When to buy

Many people would assume that time doesn't make a difference. They would believe that as long as they feel ready to buy one, they should just go and shop for an RV.

Well, the demand for RVs fluctuates throughout the year. For this reason, RVs are seasonal items. Meaning you can take advantage of the seasons. Many people love to go camping during the spring and summer months. During these months, people tend to buy more RVs. RV shops swarm during such months, and dealers are so busy; they don't have the time and patience to offer discounts.

Demand for RVs during cold winter months is always lower than in the summer and spring months. Subsequently, the late fall and winter months would be the best times to purchase, specifically October-January. During these months, RVs sell the least. Most people aren't thinking about purchasing RVs during this time, so salespeople and private vendors are desperate to get rigs off their hands. They will readily give potential buyers incentives and deep discounts. The discounts are available all across the board.

The discounts are even deeper in the north, where the weather is frigid and unsuitable for camping during fall and winter. Prices do fall everywhere, but if you live in warm states such as Texas and Florida, you typically won't get as significant of discounts.

I also recommend end-of-the-month purchases because salesmen often have a monthly quota they need to hit at the end of every month.

Insurance and Warranties

Insurance and warranties are like your wallet and keys. You can never leave home without them. Both are important, and they protect you in different ways. If you bought an electronic, you would want to purchase an extended warranty for it. The same applies to RVs. When it comes to RV protection, many travelers have trouble distinguishing between RV insurance and warranty coverage. So what's the difference between the two?

RV insurance

There is so much to explore when you are touring the country in your beloved RV, but not all surprises are good, which is why RV insurance helps.

RV insurance covers costs associated with incidents like collisions, natural disasters, and theft. Insurance protects you and your RV should something go wrong while you're out camping or when the rig is in storage. This is usually a requirement, and I highly recommend that every RV owner gets insurance.

Full-time RV insurance

Not every insurance company covers full-time RVers. This is why your agent needs to know if you plan on living in your RV for more than 150 days each year. Doing this will help you understand the impact of being a full-time RVer on your coverage. Ask lots of questions so that you don't suffer the consequences of obscure holes in your policy.

For example, does your insurance have additional liability coverage when people visit your campsite and get hurt?

Always make sure that you have roadside assistance in your insurance plan. I wouldn't feel comfortable traveling in remote locations without it.

When looking for an insurance provider, do your research and request quotes from several insurance companies. This allows you to select the one that offers the best insurance rates while also giving you the coverage you need.

Know that insurance will vary depending on the state.

Some of the best insurance companies include;

- Good Sam
- National General
- Progressive

RV warranty

An RV warranty covers the repair expenses for the components that make your RV move. Basically, an RV warranty pays for your repair bills.

It is prevalent for RVs to have major mechanical breakdowns within the first few years on the road. RV repairs are costly and time-consuming. These costs only add up as RV continues to break down.

RV warranties aren't required by law, but they help increase the resale value of your rig should you decide to sell. Having a warranty indicates that the RV was maintained correctly and will give peace of mind to any future buyers. When it comes to warranties, there are 2 types;

- **Comprehensive policy**

A comprehensive policy will list everything that is covered. This means, if something in your rig fails that isn't in the contract, it won't be covered. Comprehensive policies are usually cheaper compared to exclusionary policies.

- **Exclusionary Policy**

An exclusionary policy is the better and more expensive warranty that lists every component excluded from coverage. If the failure that occurs is not on this exclusions list, it's covered.

Warranties are very complicated. One of the most important things to consider when buying a warranty is who you buy it from. They should be trustworthy because they will be the ones going to bat for you when things go wrong.

There are many excellent warranties out there and many scams, so you have to do your research and read the fine print (you'll be surprised by some of the stuff you find). The only thing that matters is what is in print, not what the salesman says.

When looking for warranties, you don't have to buy from your dealer. There are many warranties on the market, so don't limit yourself to just one dealer.

I highly recommend buying your warranty from Wholesale Warranties because they have high ratings and impressive reviews. They offer excellent services, competitive prices and provide several options for customers to choose from.

Also, make sure many repair centers work with your warranty company. Your warranty should preferably offer nationwide service. There is nothing worse than your RV breaking down while you are hundreds of miles away from the nearest repair center that can service you.

In the end, the most important thing when you are sourcing for warranties is to READ THE FINE PRINT. Do that, and you should be fine.

3

RV TOWING

W hite knuckles. You might be familiar with them; I mean, every RVer has gone through the pain while learning how to tow. When you're new to it, towing an RV can feel pretty intimidating. It takes lots of time and energy to get comfortable with towing a rig. Here's everything you need to know to build your confidence, so you can relax and loosen your grip as you set foot on the pedal.

Towing a Vehicle

Travel trailers and fifth Wheels

If possible, buy your trailer or fifth wheel before you buy your tow vehicle. This way, you will have more freedom to choose the right house for you instead of finding a rig that works with your truck.

Terms

GVW (gross vehicle weight)-is how much the trailer and its payload weigh together.

GVWR (gross vehicle weight rating)-is the highest weight the trailer can safely and comfortably hold and transport.

Depending on your rig, you'll need to determine which type of hitch you'll need. A hitch is a point that connects to a vehicle's chassis for towing.

There are four main types of hitches:

I. Weight-carrying

This is the most basic hitch and is used for small- and medium-sized trailers. It uniformly distributes your trailer tongue loads through the bumper and frame of the tow vehicle.

You can quickly load and unload this hitch and comfortably tow medium too small-sized trailers. Always make sure the ball mount is rated to handle the weight of your trailer.

II. Weight-distributing

This hitch is designed for heavier travel trailers, as it evenly distributes the weight of your payload. It works by using adjustable spring bars and tension to distribute the trailer's weight to the tow truck's axles.

There are many benefits to a weight distribution hitches such as;

- Even weight distribution
- More trailer tow capacity
- Better control over your vehicle
- Less wear and tear on the vehicle
- Improved steering and brake control

However, they are more complicated and take longer to connect and disconnect from the truck.

I generally recommend a weight-distribution hitch for larger RVs, but you will need one if;

- The trailer's weight is equal to or exceeds 50% of the tow vehicle's GVWR
- Sagging occurs at the rear end of your tow vehicle when it is attached to the trailer
- Trailer sway is a common occurrence
- Steering or stopping your rig is a challenging task

You can choose to add sway bars to your weight distribution hitch to help reduce sway and to feel safer; however, they are not needed for every trailer.

III. Gooseneck

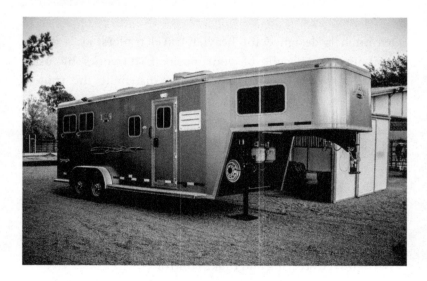

A gooseneck hitch uses a hitch ball that mounts under the truck bed and bolts onto the truck frame using brackets to connect the trailer. It allows for a tight turn radius and is mounted in the bed of a tow truck. Gooseneck hitches can pull loads as heavy as 30,000 lbs or more. The biggest advantage of using gooseneck hitches is that their mechanism is less invasive. For this reason, a complete truck bed is available for use when towing your trailer. They are well structured to tow huge loads such as flatbeds, large trailers, toy haulers, or livestock. The weight capacity of gooseneck hitches is usually higher compared to other hitches.

I would not recommend using a gooseneck for towing your 5fth wheel, but it is possible.

IV. Fifth wheel

Fifth wheel hitches are big hitches with hinged plates that sit in the bed of your tow truck. Long-bed trucks are best suited for the fifth wheel hitch. Slider fifth wheel hitches will also work perfectly with short-bed trucks.

They consist of many components and have a bulky and heavy design. A fifth-wheel towing is generally more stable, smoother, and quieter than a gooseneck hitch. It is worth noting that fifth-wheel hitches can be used on pickup trucks only. If you have a fifth-wheel travel trailer, I highly recommend this hitch over the gooseneck hitch.

Motorhome Towing

Many RVers choose to tow their car behind the motorhome because it allows them to be more mobile.

There are three main types of motorhome towing.

I. Flat Towing

Flat towing means that all four tires and wheels will be on the ground at all times. Unlike the bulky equipment needed for dolly and trailer towing, flat towing gets the job done with a small tow bar.

The flexibility of a flat tow allows you to go exploring, shopping, and sightseeing at a moment's notice with no need to drag the RV all over the city.

What you will need;

- Tow Bar
- Base plate kit installed on the tow vehicle
- Wiring kit (for lights and breaking)
- Safety cables
- Supplemental braking system

It's worth noting that you cannot back up your motorhome while the vehicle is attached. However, unhooking the toad and backing up doesn't require much time.

Ensure the manufacturer approves your vehicle before towing on all fours because many vehicle transmissions do not allow this option. You have to be extra cautious; otherwise, you will do severe damage to your tow vehicle

Installing all of this equipment is very challenging and expensive. If you are not a good mechanic, I highly recommend getting this done by a professional.

If your vehicle allows you to flat tow, I recommend this option over the others.

II. Tow Dolly

A tow dolly is a type of trailer that attaches using a ball hitch. After attaching the hitch, you drive your vehicle up onto the tow dolly. The front two wheels of a car are loaded while the car's rear wheels are on the ground rolling.

A significant advantage of using a tow dolly is that you can tow a wide variety of vehicles on a tow dolly.

With a tow dolly, you will need;

- Straps (to anchor the vehicle down)
- Safety chains

A tow dolly is used mainly for vehicles with front-wheel drive transmissions. However, rear-wheel-drive cars can use a tow dolly if their transmissions are disconnected (I would not recommend this). Tow dollies are pretty big and take up a lot of storage, but you can easily store your dolly somewhere on the campsite.

Tow dollies are heavy and can add approximately 500 – 1,000 lbs to the existing tow weight. Also, note you can't back up the motorhome while the dolly is attached. I highly recommend getting a tow dolly with brakes installed because not all of them come with brakes.

III. Car Trailer

A car trailer is a four-wheel car carrier that lifts and holds your entire vehicle off the ground. It allows you to haul the car while it's entirely on top of the trailer.

If you have an all-wheel-drive or 4-wheel drive vehicle, chances are you'll have to put it on a trailer to tow it behind your motorhome. Like the tow dolly, you can pull a wide variety of vehicles on a trailer compared to flat towing.

When using a car trailer hinge, you'll save significant wear and tear on your toad's engine and transmission while you haul it.

You will need;

- Ramps (if the trailer does not include them)
- Ratchet straps for tie-down
- Brake controller (if the trailer has electric brakes)

Due to the large size of the trailer, it can be challenging to maneuver around parking lots, gas stations, and campgrounds. Unlike the other hinges, with talented driver skills, you can back up your motorhome while the trailer/toad is attached.

The only con of using a car trailer compared to a tow dolly is the equipment's cost. It is usually more expensive than owning/renting a tow dolly. But if you are serious about driving, I recommend a car trailer over a tow dolly.

Do's and don'ts of towing

- Always use the right tools for your specific towing style
- Do lots of practice
- Never exceed the recommended weight limit
- Make sure all your towing equipment gets installed correctly

4

PLANNING YOUR FIRST TRIP

W hile it would be great to wake up and find yourself all set just a few moments away from your next climb or hike, it is never that straight-forward. To be a road warrior, you have to do some planning before you start towing your mobile home around. First, I would recommend going to an empty parking lot to practice necessary RVing skills such as parking and backing up. You may also want to spend a night or two in the driveway or a parking lot near home to get a good feel of the RV.

In this chapter, you will learn how to plan your first trip and save money while you are out on the road by utilizing apps and clubs effectively.

Planning

Maybe the word planning alone gives you anxiety and makes your eyes glaze over with apathy. Perhaps you are a committed, obsessed RV planner with personalized itineraries and agendas ideally classified for each family member. Whichever extreme you choose, one thing that stands: the art of planning must be well executed. Now, this is not to say that you should go full-on spreadsheet crazy. In fact, most people appreciate the flexibility of living in an RV. Your first trip will set the tone for how you feel about RVing, so it's best to keep it simple. I recommend going to a simple, pleasant, and scenic place that is close to home.

A great way to plan your route is to set a limit on how much driving you want to do in a day. If you want to enjoy a nice, relaxed speed, aim for a 4-6 hour drive per day. Be sure to include some extra time for detours as well. Always be realistic with your driving goals and stay on the safe side.

If you set up a camp close to your house, the territory will be very familiar. Plus, if you forget something important, you're not far from home. If you opt for a campsite, make sure you've booked your spot far in advance. The best national and state parks are usually booked well ahead of time, especially during the summer and holiday seasons, so I recommend you act early. It's the worst feeling when you show up to a fully booked campground that won't take you. Do your research and read online reviews of your chosen campsite to see if it is good.

Types of campsites

Every RVer has a unique idea of what the perfect RVing trip should be. For some, it's setting camp in the middle of nowhere, surrounded by the serenity of nature. Others see RVs as a home away from home as they travel the world. Still, others believe it is all about sightseeing or staying put in one place. No matter which option you pick, there is a real chance you aren't fully aware of how many camping options are available.

Every RVer has a unique idea of what the perfect RVing trip should be. For some, it's setting camp in the middle of nowhere, surrounded by the serenity of nature. Others see RVs as a home away from home as they travel the world. Still, others believe it is all about sightseeing or staying put in one place. No matter which option you pick, There are two types of campsites when it comes to parking.

- Pull through sites - Allow rigs to drive forward through the site entrance and continue pulling forward to exit the site.

- Back in sites- require the driver to back into the campsite.

Angling a trailer in a spot shouldn't be one of your worries as a beginner. On your first trip, please try and find a simple pull-thru site. Once you are in position, you can connect your RV to hookups such as water, electricity, and sewers. Find a site that is level to the ground. A good level campsite provides excellent stability for you and the camper. Your preferred campsite should have amenities, such as a swimming pool, washrooms, and campfires.

If you are worried about your rig's length, then measuring it should be something on your mind. With the proper measurements, you can reserve a site that fits your RV well. If you have a trailer, make sure the tow vehicle's length is included in the measurement.

Take note of cancellation policies, and make sure you have them documented along with your reservation dates. If anything changes while you are on your trip, you will be well prepared.

Things to consider when choosing a campground;

- Amenities offered
- Discounts offered
- Check-in time
- Late arrival policy
- Are full hookups (water, electricity, etc.) available?
- The size of the site

Outline your route

All successful road trips must start with a vision. Just like snowflakes, no two trips are the same. The goal is to create an exciting trip where the scenic highways give you as much adventure as the destination. The structure of your road trip matters; you can manipulate the itinerary so that cities and attractions become the foundation. Whether you choose to drive through the major cities or go deep into the country, you must outline your route well. Once you have an idea of where and when you want to go on your first trip, its time to make the outline.

As you are outlining, look out for propane restrictions and low clearance tunnels and bridges. Look out for switchbacks and steep grades that may be challenging to navigate while driving your RV.

Think of your options carefully and check for the following;

- Are there any steep inclines or declines, narrow roads, and low bridges along your path?
- Should you be expecting any tolls along the way?
- Are there rest stops along the route?
- Does the route take or avoid congested city roads?

RV Apps

Traveling in the digital age is super-cool. We have a wide range of mobile apps at our disposal. Throughout my travels, I have used my fair share of these great apps. Here are some of my favorite apps that I use to find the best hiking trails, free dispersed campgrounds, check the weather, and connect with other travelers.

- **All Stays**

In my opinion, this is the best RV app. In addition to 30,000 campgrounds, the app lets users search for retail stores, parking, truck stops (with fuel prices listed), rest areas, RV stores, and more. As you drive, the map continually refreshes to show locations that fall within your filters, making it easy to plan on the go. This app is $9.99, and it more than pays for itself.

- **Campendium**

Campendium is a great free app that helps you find campgrounds. This app has user-generated reviews that provide valuable details and helpful information. For example, it shows photos of the campground and tells you how strong cell coverage around the park is.

- **RV Parks and a Campgrounds**

This app helps people find great RV Parks across the USA, Canada, and Mexico. The parks are sorted by rating and can be viewed in list mode. This free app is great if you don't know where to start your RV adventure.

- ***GasBuddy***

GasBuddy is an excellent free app that helps you plan your fuel stops. This app helps you find fuel stops close to you while displaying fuel prices. It might not seem like a lot; however, you can save up to $340 a year on gas using this app through the discounts provided. You can also use this app when you are not RVing.

- **Accu Weather**

This app will give you updates on daily and hourly forecasts. It provides you information on potential severe weather and the air quality around you. You are free to customize the app for more relevant forecasts and weather updates based on the places you plan to visit.

- **Yelp**

This is a great free app that helps you find reviews from locals and distant RVers. This app is great for finding the best restaurants anywhere. These reviews are not always the most reliable; however, you can never go wrong with Yelp.

- **Roadtrippers**

Roadtrippers has answers to all your questions about where to stop while you are on your trip. The app will help you locate parks, roadside attractions, and scenic points. You can get up to seven waypoints on the free version.

These apps make life so much easier and will allow you to plan efficient RV routes.

Preparing your RV

Before you go anywhere…..

- Ensure your RV is in prime condition.
- Book a service appointment and ensure the tires, oil, air filters, and fluids are checked.
- Ensure the lights and blinkers are working correctly, and you have an extra tire if anything happens.
- Carry up-to-date copies of your insurance cards and registration documents.
- Know your safety kit has all the necessary equipment and extras, such as a flashlight, jumper cables, and reflective triangles.
- Significant phone numbers and membership information should be kept in a place you can access easily.
- Carry a spare charger and keys just in case something happens to them.
- If your RV is a rental, make sure you understand the driving regulations, the allocated mileage, and emergency contact information. You will find these on the rental agreement.

Take it slow

RVs are not like your average sedan. Just looking at them tells you this much. They take longer to slow down, speed up, and break. You have to be gentle while driving an RV.

Never get into a hurry; this is where mistakes are made. One of the most common mistakes new RV road-trippers make is expecting to move at the same pace as a regular car. That's not going to happen, so reasonable expectations when planning your itinerary are important. You have to take a different approach when driving an RV because it takes way more focus and energy than driving a car. An easy rule of thumb is to plan an average route speed of 50 miles per hour.

ALWAYS do a walkaround inspection before moving your RV. You can damage your rig severely if you leave a power cord in or your trailer is not attached correctly.

On your first trip, try not to drive too much in one day. It's best to start your drive early so that you can move in the daylight. Driving at night can be very dangerous. Besides, finding help in case of an accident or an injury would be hard, if not impossible. Most RV dealerships, garages, and auto part stores are closed during the night.

For example, just the other day, I got locked out of my RV, and it was 11 at night. I looked, and all the major roadside assistance companies were closed. Being a genius, I decided to call the one 24-hour roadside assistance company called Minute Key that had 0 reviews (red flag). Little did I know this was a complete scam, and I lost 75 dollars. Scamming stranded drivers that need roadside assistance is actually a huge thing. So be very careful if you ever find yourself stranded at night. Sometimes I wish I followed my own advice. Don't drive late at night.

Find a community

Having a good community makes RVing ten times more enjoyable. RV travelers are some of the friendliest people in the world. Most RVers are excited and eager to connect with other RVers, so don't be shy. To tell you the truth, I have met some of my best friends on the road. As a beginner RVer, you are not going to know how to do everything. You can always ask for help from other experienced RVers. Those expert RVers you see now were in your shoes, and most of them are always more than happy to help.

Besides walking out of the campground and approaching new people, here are some great ways to get connected with RVers.

Internet community

The internet is a great place to connect with fellow RV enthusiasts.

Some place to connect with RVers include;

Facebook groups

They are great for helping you stay connected with other RVers. Here are a few examples;

- **How to RV for Newbies**

For new RV owners who want advice from seasoned RVers.

- **Full-time RV Families**

This group helps you find other families on the road, and they host regular meetups across the country.

- **Frugal Full-Time RVers**

Great for RVers who are passionate about boondocking.

- **The Rv Entrepreneur**

This community helps each other solve cellular connectivity issues, bounce around business ideas and share valuable articles about nomadic work.

- **The RV Bunch**

A good light-hearted community that posts all kinds of RV information.

RV clubs

The number of RVers has skyrocketed in just a few years. Clubs and organizations have blossomed to meet the demands of these travel enthusiasts. Even older organizations have expanded their reach and included clubs as part of their programs. RV clubs are great, and most cost anywhere from $30 to $100. However, they often offer discounts to different camp-sites and parks. If you join the right club, you will end up saving money because of the available discounts. They also keep you updated and allow you to be a part of an RV community.If you are serious about RVing, I recommend joining a club or two.

Some great clubs include;

- **RV Village**

Is great for those looking to stay connected with RVing friends after meeting them or those who want to meet new people though planned meetups.

- **North American Family Campers Association**

This club hosts many events for RVers. Both expert and amateur RVers can meet and learn from each other during the events.

- **Family Campers and RVers**

An excellent club for campers who want to enjoy a few offers on several products and services related to RVing and have access to exclusive RV events.

- $35 for 1 year
- $68 for 2 years
- $99 for 3 years
- $560 for lifetime membership

- **RVing women**

A group made just for RV women. These women share advice and exciting travel stories during their rallies .

- **Instagram**

Instagram is a great platform to reach out and meet other RVers just like you. There are so many RVers on Instagram, and you are bound to find some groups you like. Search for popular hashtags such as #rving or #rvlife to find them.

There are so many great RV clubs and apps out there; however, these will allow you to connect with the most people and build up your community. I will go over clubs that have other benefits later in the chapter.

Know things are going to go wrong

Living in an RV is the ultimate lifestyle, and rightfully so because it comes with so many benefits. But challenges do exist, especially on the maiden trip. Things will not always go as planned.

As it is, towing or driving a recreational vehicle is mentally exhausting. You have to be alert at all times, always one step ahead. It gets tiring looking around and calculating radiuses, judging the stopping distance accurately, and keeping a constant watch of anything on either side of the rig. All these can cause mental fatigue, so you need to be prepared.

This is the mindset you should have as you start your journey. That way, if something goes wrong, you won't panic, and if nothing goes wrong, then perfect. RVing is easier if you are well prepared to deal with any eventuality.

Here are some challenges you should be prepared for;

- **Changing weather**

No matter where you are in the country, the weather will always be a factor. It will not always cooperate with your calendar, so you need to be prepared and informed. RVs aren't built like homes; they can lose lots of heat and air conditioning. This means that you can wake up cold and frosty during winter even though the heating is on. Since you are moving from one state to the next, keeping up with the weather may become a little challenging.

If you find yourself in a tornado (worst case scenario), take extreme caution; RVs are more prone to winds than ordinary cars. Make sure you know where to take refuge and familiarize yourself with all the necessary shelter locations and emergency protocols around you.

- **Injury or illness**

You are more prone to injury and illness on the road than when you are at home. Make sure to always prepare for the worst-case scenario. Carry a fast aid kit and replenish or replace any expired supplies.

- **Break down**

This is one of the most common challenges you will most likely experience on the road. You should have insurance and road-side assistance which is usually part of the insurance coverage. A good warranty and insurance plan will have you back on the road within no time without draining your wallet.

- **Theft**

As an RV owner, you stand out, making you a target for thieves. You can take a few simple precautions to protect your belongings. Always keep your travel paraphernalia and luggage out of sight. Make sure to keep things hidden; most RV theft occurs when valuables get left in plain sight.

- **Tickets**

Avoid tickets as much as you can. They can really add up over time.

Full-time RVing isn't any different from any other type of life-style. It comes with its fair share of benefits and challenges. While the lifestyle is a little different, its relevance remains. Going into this lifestyle without acknowledging these challenges sets you up for failure. Hopefully, the list above prepares you and helps you keep an open mind.

Cost of RV traveling

- **Budget**

What is the cost of RV traveling?

This is probably the most asked question I get. It is also one of the most difficult questions to answer. Everyone lives differently and makes unique decisions based on preferences. Some people blowdry after every shower; others watch football all weekend, while others don't watch TV at all. Do you prefer to eat at home? Or do you eat out every day? Most RVers appreciate the community and socialization at camp, while a few would rather enjoy their peace and solitude alone, in the middle of nowhere. All these decisions are fine, but you get the picture. You must understand that the costs associated with RVing change depending on what you choose.

Generally, RVing can be very expensive, which is why I highly recommend creating a budget before you depart on your adventure. RV travel has very many variables, so quoting an exact budget figure would be a little tricky.

The cost will depend on the activities you have planned, the campgrounds you reserved, and the length of your trip.

So how do you estimate your costs and save money while you are on the road? The first thing to do is to break down all of your trip-related expenses by category.

On the road you will have three main expenses;

Travel

- Gas
- RV rental fee
- Propane and generator fuel
- Excursions
- Tolls

Food

- Eating out
- Groceries

Fees

- Campground fees
- National Park fees
- Laundry fees
- Dumping fees
- Storage fees
- Maintenance and repair fees
- Internet fees

As you can see, there are many expenses to pay for in your everyday RV life. Work out your travel budget based on your preferences and financial constraints. Always make sure to track your expenses because RVing is very expensive. Having a budget on traveling fees gives you peace of mind knowing that you can financially sustain this lifestyle.

How to save money on the road

I may not be a financial expert, but I have met and heard from many people who are living this lifestyle and saving money while at it. If there is one important lesson I have learned, it's how important living within your means is. If you don't learn how to live within your budget, you will always be stressed out. No matter how much money you have or make, you will always need more. Look at your lifestyle and your spending choices. If cash is a problem right now, should you buy a brand new RV? Should you pay $100 for cable TV? You have to figure out your budget, plan around it and save while on the road. Here are some tips for saving money on your voyage.

Eat at home

Trying out new restaurants and all the places people highly recommend can be tempting. However, you can save a lot of money when you decide to eat at home. Eating in more often will save you a fortune. Not to mention it is typically better for you.

Staying Put

If you're not in a rush, one of the best ways to save money is by staying in one place for a long time. You will save a lot of money on fuel as well as campground costs. This also allows you to work around a monthly campground rate which is cheaper than weekly or daily rates. You are on this lifestyle to travel, but it doesn't have to be a sprint. Stay for a while and soak in the beautiful location.

Activities

Try out activities such as hiking, biking, and kayaking that are exciting but free. This way, you can reduce the costs of side excursions.

APPS and MEMBERSHIPS

- ***Passport America***

Cost

- $44 a year
- $79 for two years
- $109 for three years

This membership offers 50% off nightly camping rates for over 1,800 campsites across North America. When you use this membership, READ THE FINE PRINT because every campground has different criteria for when the discount is available. Passport America will quickly pay for itself within two to three nights of using it. This membership is a no-brainer whether you are a full-time traveler or weekend warrior.

Pro tip

Make sure passport America supports the campground you want to visit during the time you are visiting. Passport America often only offers discounts during a certain time of the year for some campgrounds.

Harvest Hosts

Cost

- $99 a year

This membership allows you to enjoy unique camping opportunities all over the US and Canada. You will have access to 1,700 fun places to stay, such as bowling alleys, farms, wineries, and even museums.

Harvest Hosts cost $99 a year; however, there is security if you don't like it. A 3-month 100% money-back guarantee if you are not impressed with the membership.

The guidelines advise members to limit themselves to a one-night stay per host. Still, you can always stay longer if the host invites you. This membership is great if you enjoy boondocking and staying in adventurous places as you go from campground to campground. I would only recommend this membership if you plan to RVing across the country for an extended time.

Chambers of commerce and welcome centers

Each state has a welcome center. They provide useful maps of the state and state park guides in every welcome center. You will also learn the most exciting and popular sites for each state. Use the information you find in welcome centers as reference points to make your plan.

The chambers of commerce are also good places to visit. Chambers provide extra information on local attractions and sites. Ask what type of activities and products they offer. You can get great stuff such as coupon books which you can use in restaurants and attraction sites. This allows you to save a lot of money and have a great time in the welcome centers.

Maintenance

Knowing how to do some routine maintenance tasks will help you save a lot of money while on the road. Learning some simple skills such as changing a tire and patching a leak in the roof will pay off in the long run.

Other tasks such as replacing your sewer vent may even sound intimidating at first. Still, they are usually not near as complicated as they seem. If you learn how to do these things yourself, you will save lots of time and money.

Try saving on gas

RVs burn way more gas than regular vehicles. This ends up being more and more costly over time. You can keep the gas guzzle at bay using a few tips;

•**Drive slowly**- You're already driving slowly for safety reasons, but it will save you a lot of gas. For every 5 mph faster than 60 that you drive, your gas mileage decreases up to 7 percent.

•**Empty your tanks**-Always keep your tanks empty until you get to the camping location. Apart from keeping enough water for the bathroom and other necessities, empty the tanks as frequently as possible—the extra weight results in more fuel consumption.

•**Try not to drive on windy days**- Driving an RV on windy days is outright terrifying and exhausting. Your engine has to work extra hard because of the extra resistance. Eventually, it consumes more gallons of fuel; if you can avoid it, great!

Volunteer or Workcamp

If you are volunteering or work-camping, you could cut your camping costs significantly. Work-camping is where you substitute work hours for camping. Check out such opportunities on workamper.com.

You can also volunteer to work on historic sites and national parks in exchange for camping.

Change your residency

If you are a full-time RVer, changing your place of residency can save you a lot of money. Every RVer has a different financial situation, and this strategy wouldn't fit everyone.

However, if you still earn money while on the road full-time, you can change your residency and opt for a state where the income tax is less.

You could also minimize other costs such as property taxes, ancillary fees, and auto & RV insurance. Seek professional advice from a tax accountant before you make this move.

Shoulder Season

Shoulder season describes a time or season when a specific location has the least number of visitors. You will enjoy lower prices and smaller crowds during the off-season. Of course, shoulder seasons exist for specific reasons. Maybe the weather isn't as conducive, or it's not the most convenient time for families with kids to travel. Take advantage of the "Shoulder Season" if your schedule allows it and the weather doesn't scare you.

5

GETTING YOUR RV READY FOR THE VOYAGE

ven as a little boy, I was obsessed with the idea of traveling across the U.S. The thought of driving along classic highways in my father's rig, blasting cool tunes, and enjoying all the pitstops along the way always made me excited. I was always obsessed with the thought of collecting polaroids and memories as we visited one site after another. My parents would worry about RV trip planning and packing back in the day. All I had to do was show up, sit pretty, and enjoy the trip. And now here I am, doing it all on my own. I am still looking to create fun memories, build campfires, watch amazing sunsets, and ride on dusty mountain roads. It feels like a bucket list dream that has been made even more accessible with the growing movement of RV life.

But one thing indeed remains; the challenges of having to pack every time we set on our next trip. It's always a dilemma. What should I pack, what should I leave behind, and how can I maximize my storage space while staying within the acceptable weight limits? Whether a novice or a veteran, packing for an RV trip needs some good forethought and planning. While your rig may seem like it has endless cabinets, nooks, shelves, and crannies, you will soon find out that the space is minimal. You will have to figure out a way to make the most of the available room. There's nothing as overwhelming as frantically trying to round up your family before leaving on that first trip. Like every family, it tends to get a little chaotic when you pack the morning of the trip, and you can forget a lot. The list of things you need to pack might seem endless, but the process doesn't have to be stressful or intimidating.

Start by making a list of all the essential things you need based on your daily needs. In this chapter, you will learn how to pack effectively for your first-ever trip. I will also share a few tips on how to get the internet up and running on the road.

Packing List

These are some items I always pack;

Kitchen

• Utensils

• Plates or Paper plates

• Cups

• Measuring cups

• Measuring spoons

• Mixing Spoons

• Spatulas

• Tongs

• Pots

• Skillets

- Oven pans

- Mixing bowls

- Colander

- Cutting Board

- Oven mitts

- Food Scale

- Wine Bottle opener

- Wine stopper

- Can opener

- Tupperware

- Food clips

- Ziploc Bags

- Tinfoil

- Napkins

- Saran wrap

- Cooler

- Water bottles (Try to reuse these)

Appliances

- Blender

- Coffee Maker

- Toaster

Cleaning supplies

- Trash bags

- Paper towels

- Cloth Towels

- Dish Soap

- Dish Rack

- Sponge

- Windex

- Air freshener

- Disinfecting wipes

- Laundry detergent

- Laundry Basket

- Broom

- Mop

Bathroom

- Shampoo

- Conditioner

- Body wash

- Shaving Cream

- Razors

- Toothbrush

- Toothpaste

- Mouthwash

- Floss

- Deodorant

- Hand soap

- RV friendly Toilet paper (yes, you need special toilet paper) I'll go over this next chapter

- Sunscreen

- Bug spray *

- Lotion

- Towels

- Beach towels

- Hairbrush

- Hair products

- Hair Dryer

- Hair Ties

- Nail Clippers

- Tissues

- First Aid kit

- Medications

Living room

• Books

• Clock

• Speaker

• Candles

• Lighter

• Pictures

Office

• Printer

• Paper

• Pens

• Pencils

• Notebooks/journals

• Tape

• Scissors

• Ruler

• Tape Measure

• Laptop

• Hard Drives

• USB Cords

• Laptop Charger

• Batteries

• any other work supplies you want/ need

Bedroom

- Sheets
- Pillows
- Blankets
- Mattress topper *
- Fans
- Phone Charger
- Hamper

Outdoor Items

- Camera
- Camping Chairs
- Binoculars
- Wood
- Grill
- Hiking shoes
- Bicycles
- Frisbee
- Kites
- Bucket
- Pocket knife

Mechanical Gear

- Surge Protector
- Electrical Adaptor

- Leveling Blocks
- Wheel Chocks
- Tire Pressure Gauge
- 50/30 amp adaptor
- Extensions chords
- Electrical duct tape
- Drinking water hose
- Water Filter
- Sewer hose
- Work gloves
- Rubber gloves
- Shovel
- Propane
- Jumper cables
- Spare tires
- Toolbox

I'll go over what all this stuff does in the next chapter.

Important documents

- Passport
- Vehicle Registration
- Insurance Paperwork
- Tax Files
- Maintenance Records

Clothing

There is no magic number of clothes that you need. It all depends on your situation. People always overpack their closet with everything they own, and it's just a waste of space. Only pack clothes that you love and know you are going to wear. It is also important that you have versatile garments that you can wear in different climates.

This list is by no means exhaustive. It is just a simple guide that will help you as you start packing for your RV trip. The most important advice is that you should never overpack. There is only so much space in an RV. Go for multi-functional, light-weight, and small items as much as you can. You'd be surprised how little you can live off of.

For example, pack one lid for a frying pan and cooking pan that uses the same lid size. Carry mixing bowls that can transform into serving bowls too. Bring items that can be used on multiple dishes. You can even do some prep work such as cutting and separating or marinating and seasoning at home before you set off on your trip.

You may experience bumpy roads once in a while, and things can get messy. Leave your breakables at home. It's annoying having to clean up broken glass on the road(trust me). If you find that you are still exceeding the maximum weight even after removing all the unnecessary items, consider starting your trip with empty water tanks. Water is usually weighty, and you can always fill up the tanks when you arrive at your destination.

Why safety should always come first when packing

While packing, you should never overlook the need for optimal RV safety. RVs are equipped with unique homelike features, but they are just vehicles at the end of the day. They must be well balanced for safe movement along the road.

Don't make the mistake of packing your RV lopsided; loads tend to shift when traveling. Trust me; you don't want your RV to sway or, in extreme cases, flip over. Keep the bottom side heavy, and don't forget to distribute the items uniformly throughout the RV.

Comfort and safety are everything while you are traveling, so make sure everything gets correctly set up. Read your manual to understand how much weight the axle can accommodate comfortably. Try and find the right balance between minimalist and well-packed.

Outside storage

Most RVs have extra storage space on the outside. This is where you will store things like sewer hoses, gloves, and sewer hose fittings. Always keep such items separate from the freshwater hose, ideally in another storage space.

Don't forget other important items such as leveling blocks and wheel chocks – both get used when parking an RV. Other outdoor storage items include a toolkit, extra bulbs, and spare fuses. You can also carry outdoor cooking gear, a patio mat, and fold-up patio furniture if you have extra space.

6

RV INTERNET

RV traveling is great, but if you need an internet connection, you better come up with a plan. Nowadays, a stable internet connection is necessary, whether you want to work on the road, have access to emergency contacts in remote locations, or stay in touch with loved ones.

How can we share our adventures with family and friends? My kids are obsessed with Fortnite and Minecraft. How can we watch YouTube videos such as *The RVers* or *RVgeeks* on the road? Can I maintain a professional and desirable professional reputation while on the road?

These are some of the internet-related questions most RV travelers like to ask. After all, internet connection has become a way of life.

Individual internet connection varies from one RVer to another, but everyone has some connection needs. Many factors such as cost, length of travel, and destination will affect your internet access while on the road.

Determining the right plan

- The first thing you need to think about is how fast the internet needs to be?
- Do you plan on working from your RV?
- Do you want to check social media and your emails only?
- Are you traveling in a remote area?
- Is entertainment a priority – Hulu, Netflix, and video games?

Suppose you only plan on using the internet occasionally. You can probably make good use of Wi-Fi available at the campground or a mobile hotspot from your phone. However, many RVers need a better connection than the campground Wi-Fi or free Mcdonald's Wi-Fi. You also may need to consider unlimited data if you are streaming movies, doing zoom calls, or things like homeschooling are vital to you. Most people don't realize how fast 30 Gb of data goes by when you stream it, especially when traveling with a family.

If you want to learn more than you ever could possibly know about mobile internet, check out

rvmobileinternet.com.

They have the best resources and continue to test everything related to mobile internet.

I. Campground Wi-Fi

Campground Wi-Fi is the easiest and cheapest way to get an internet connection while traveling in an RV. However, you shouldn't expect much when you are using campground Wi-Fi. Campground Wi-Fi is famous for being overcrowded and notoriously slow. Besides, you never really know what you are going to get, especially during peak season. You may get a connection that is strong enough for streaming services, but this is extremely rare. Again, hacking is a real threat because the internet connection isn't secure. If you are not getting a good connection on the campground, the alternative could be free Wi-Fi in places like McDonald's and Starbucks. Public Wi-Fi allows you to check or reply to your emails, do the necessary downloads and uploads, send pictures to your family members and check your socials.

You can also take advantage of free Wi-Fi in coffee shops and libraries. Free Wi-Fi is the best option if you travel occasionally or on the weekends only.

Pros of public Wi-Fi

- It is free
- It is widely available, especially near cities
- Easy to access

Cons of public Wi-Fi

- The quality isn't ideal
- Not secure
- Overcrowded
- Too slow

Safety tips for using public Wi-Fi

- Try using VPN (Virtual Private Network) as much as possible. This way, you can protect your private information by encrypting any data sent to and from your device. Free VPNs exist, but they might not be as safe. You may have to pay for an effective VPN.
- Always turn off AirDrop and file sharing on your devices when you are on public Wi-Fi. Hackers always use these two avenues because they are easily accessible.
- Your interaction should be limited to sites that have enough security to protect your information. Here's how to know; look out for the address "HTTPS." The "S" shows that the network is secure, and the information sent back and forth will be protected.
- Google chrome always sends an alert if a connection isn't secure, but you can take caution on your own. If your business is very important and sensitive, you may not want to use public Wi-Fi.

Wi-Fi Booster

The signal might be feeble at the campground, but you can improve the connection. The access point is the most crucial part of any Wi-Fi connection because that's where the signal originates.

You may not be able to move or improve on the access point because it may be out of reach. The only way is to improve your receiver/transmitter. This is where Wi-Fi boosters come in. Wi-Fi boosters have a powerful antenna that can receive weak signals from all over the campground.

The antennae sits on your RV's roof, pulling signals from the access point to you.

As you can imagine, Wi-Fi boosters only work with Wi-Fi signals. You can not use them on cellular towers.

II. Cellular Data

RV campgrounds can tout their connection all day long, but when it gets real, even the best Wi-Fi plans can disappoint. Fortunately, you can opt for a mobile hotspot with your cell signal provider. If you can't function without the internet, you will most likely need an unlimited cellular plan. This plan works by purchasing a hotspot device from a data provider such as AT&T, Verizon, or T-Mobile.

Mobile Hotspot (MiFi/JetPack)

A hotspot device will let you stream movies, download files, and facetime family members. It takes a cellular connection and converts it into a data connection. This creates a local area network that you can connect to. You can try to use your phone as a hotspot; however, the hotspot device works so much better.

When choosing a hotspot provider, you can't go wrong with the big three providers: Verizon, At&t, and T-mobile. If you already use Verizon for your phones, I recommend using At&T or Tmobile for your hotspot device and vice versa. Having multiple hotspot providers allows you to stay connected in more regions across North America. Mobile hotspot devices range anywhere from $100-200 and can do everything your home Wi-Fi can, except you can use it everywhere.

If you are worried about coverage in certain areas, you can see reviews of campsites on Campendium.com. These reviews will let you know how many bars of signal you will get from each provider, depending on your location filters. Cellular plans are pretty expensive, but they will give you a reliable connection on the road in most cases.

When looking for one of these plans, don't just walk into the local provider's store and ask for recommendations. They might give you a plan, but they aren't trained to sell internet plans to RVers. Before walking in or calling your provider, you need to know the type of plan you want and how many gigs you need a month. Too many times, I see RVers who have unlimited plans hit their cap and get slowed down to unusable internet speeds.

The cellular data option is excellent if you plan on traveling for an extended period and want a good internet connection.

Pros of cellular data

- You will have access to good internet in most places throughout the states
- You can access multiple cellular data plans. This gives you more nationwide coverage

Cons of using cellular data

- You will only have cellular data in areas your provider covers
- If you exceed a certain amount of data usage, you will be subjected to throttling, even in an "unlimited" plan
- High price

Cellular Data for R.V. Wi-Fi access

Not all devices you use will connect to cellular data directly. Tablets, streaming devices, video game consoles, and laptops can only use a Wi-Fi connection. Don't worry; there are multiple ways to bridge the gap when you are in places without Wi-Fi access.

- **Tethering and hotspot**

Most RVers use this option to connect their cellular data with other devices. Most smartphones can easily hotspot and tether to your devices. You can either use a USB cable or Wi-Fi to connect them to your cellular data.

Always check with your service provider and make sure hot-spotting is allowed (some plans don't allow hot-spotting). Start by turning the hotspot on your mobile device and connect your devices to the Wi-Fi connection broadcasted.

This wireless connection is accessible to all devices within range. You may want to protect yourself using a password so that the connection is accessible to you only. One of the main advantages of using hotspots is that the connection is more secure than public Wi-Fi.

- **Cellular Router**

Cellular routers are very sophisticated. They can either have single or multiple cellular modems. It can provide internet connection in multiple ways, such as serial connection, ethernet, and Wi-Fi.

Through either wired or local wireless connections, cellular routers provide an internet source through which your devices can easily connect. They are very versatile, and they differ in terms of prices and function.

For example, some cellular routers allow for up to 4 SIM cards. This way, you can easily use different plans on one router. It automatically selects the plan with the best coverage allowing you to enjoy the best internet connection in any particular location.

It can also spread out your internet usage across the multiple networks you are using so that you can easily avoid exhausting a single plan. Furthermore, cellular routers aggregate links (bonding), which means they can bind multiple connections into one big, fast connection that works better than the individual connections.

And while cellular routers are very cool, it is overkill for most RVers. Even with the full-time work and travel that needs speedy internet connection, cellular routers are a little excessive.

III. Satellite

A satellite connection is a solid and great choice, especially in hard-to-reach areas because the signal comes from above. Satellite connection is fast as long as you have a clear path to the sky. You will experience high latency(which means slower speeds) if your location is obstructed from obstacles or trees.

Satellite internet is pretty costly because you will be looking at hundreds of dollars on equipment and costs (both monthly and upfront).

They are extremely vulnerable to bad weather because the satellite dish has to be installed on the RV. This means your satellite will be outdoors 24/7.

HughesNet and Viasat are the two primary satellite providers in the US. Their plan doesn't cut you off when you reach your limit, but the speed may not be as fast.

Always remember that not all satellite providers offer internet services. The signals don't work well in areas with many trees and may not be very efficient for certain streaming services.

It's also common to experience lag and annoying buffering. Satellite is not always something you can rely on when you are on the go; after all, they don't work efficiently with highway airspeeds. You must take extra caution and time to set it up once you get to your destination.

Keep in mind that most satellite services offer better rates for long-term contracts. The future of the internet lies in satellites. It is an excellent option if you plan on staying in remote areas where cellular data may be a problem. As of now, I would always recommend cellular data over satellite because it is faster and cheaper.

Pros of satellite

- Works well in remote areas
- It is the future of internet

Cons

- Costly compared to other plans
- It is a cumbersome option considering the size and manual dish setup in every campsite.
- It is slow compared to cellular data and Wi-Fi

Global Internet

If you are camping outside of the U.S I recommend getting a Skyroaming device. This device is specifically designed for international travelers.

The Skyroam is very similar to a hotspot device. There are many different plans that Skyroam offer, and it shouldn't be hard finding one that fits your needs. You can purchase monthly subscriptions, buy a gigabyte of data, or buy an unlimited 24-hour data plan.

Skyroam is great; however, it isn't near as powerful as Verizon or AT&T hotspots. You can still access American cellular network services in Canada and Mexico, so I recommend global internet if you plan to travel outside of North America.

Pros of global internet

- Works well for RVers going outside North America

Cons

- The coverage offered isn't as good as the US cell phone data plans

Extra Accessories Wi-Fi Extender/Repeater/Booster

If you plan on using Wi-Fi often, you may want to invest in a Wi-Fi Extender. This device extends the range of the RV park Wi-Fi, which gives you a stronger signal in your rig. A Wi-Fi booster can cost anywhere from 50-300 dollars, and they are very easy to set up. Wi-Fi boosters won't fix all your internet problems; however, it is more helpful than harmful.

This device is suitable if;

- You are too far away to connect to the Wi-Fi
- There are obstacles between you and the Wi-Fi router
- You are experiencing a slow internet connection

This device does not;

- Make the existing Wi-Fi better

The caveat is a Wi-Fi booster can only boost the signal it's receiving. If the speed at the source is slow or everyone at the

RV park is logging on simultaneously, you're going to have a slow connection. Some of the top brands of boosters include

- Netgear
- Winegard
- Google

All of these brands create quality extenders that will get the job done. If you plan on using Wi-Fi often, this is well worth the upfront investment. Extenders are great; however, they can't fix a poor Wi-Fi signal. If you need a stable internet connection on the road, stick to cellular, especially if you plan on working from your rig.

Cell Booster

You can use a cellphone signal booster (amplifier or repeater) to boost your internet connection. A cellular booster is a device that you can purchase for around 500 dollars to help you get a better signal to your device. It has an amplifier, external and internal antennae. These three components form a wireless system that improves the strength of the phone signal and cellular reception.

By locating, amplifying, and broadcasting the cell signal, you can enjoy better cellular data on all your devices. Using a cell booster properly will allow you to create a stronger signal within a small area (aka your RV).

Cellular boosters are great;

- In fringe or areas with weak signal
- When trying to overcome obstacles that may be between you and the tower
- If upload speed is essential for your activities

They do not help if;

- You are using an overloaded tower
- You are trying to improve an already good signal
- You have gone over your data plan

MIMO

In short, MIMO (Multiple in Multiple out) is a method used by 4G LTE and 5G signals to multiply the capacity of a connection by using multiple antennas to send and receive signals. MIMO antennas range anywhere from 30-50 dollars and are very easy to install. MIMO is very versatile, and some models are directional while others are omnidirectional.

To my surprise, this cheap device outperforms cellular boosters in almost all categories except for distance and upload speed. Unlike Cellular boosters, MIMO has the potential to double your cellular speeds because it has multiple antennas. It would take me all day to explain to you the science of why; however, rvmobileinternet.com does a phenomenal job explaining why this device performs so well.

The most popular brand for RVers is the Netgear MIMO antennas. There is nothing special about the Netgear antennas; however, they are very consistent and get the job done for a low price. With MIMO, you can achieve great results for around 50 dollars. I recommend trying out MIMO antennas before investing in a 500-dollar cellular booster. MIMO is my favorite internet device on the market because you get the most bang for your buck.

Cell Phone Plans

When it comes to cell phone service, you will need a plan with nationwide coverage. The three big providers that offer this coverage include Version, At&T, and Tmobile. There are so many plans that work for so many different people; you just have to find one that fits you. The best cell phone network will depend on where you want to travel and how much you are willing to spend?

No single network works perfectly in all locations. Each has its advantages and disadvantages in different areas of the country. Try your best to figure out the combination that gives you excellent coverage and data in places you want to visit.

- **Verizon**

Verizon has the broadest reach across the United States, with 70% nationwide coverage. It is the most consistent and reliable provider out of the big three. Because of this, you will have to pay more for Verizon, but it does have the best rural coverage, and many of their plans come with perks such as free Disney plus, ESPN plus, and Apple Music.

- **AT&T**

AT&T has the second-best reach across the states, with 68% coverage. It may be the second to Verizon, but I have found that the speeds are generally similar to or faster than Verizon.

AT&T's plans sit right in the middle, giving you good coverage and decent perks at a fair price. As of now, this is my favorite provider out of the three.

- **T-mobile**

A few years ago, Verizon and AT&T used to be the two big dawgs; however, T-Mobile is making a strong resurgence. It merged with Sprint and now has a 62% coverage rate. If you plan on traveling to Canada or Mexico, T-Mobile's international should be your first choice because it blows every other carrier out of the water.

T-Mobile is the cheapest provider and has some of the best plans, providing good coverage in most areas. The only disadvantage is that many RVers love going off-grid, where T-Mobile service does not reach.

If you want a 24/7 internet connection, I recommend Verizon, AT&T, or T-Mobile for your cell plan and one of the other big three providers for your internet plan. This way, you will have a more consistent connection throughout the country.

I wish I could just recommend the best plans on the market; however, they change all the time. Once again, rvmobileinternet.com is the savior, and they go over the best RV plans quarterly. As long as you know what you want and do your research, finding a good cell phone and internet plan should be a breeze.

Researching cellular before you arrive

Even if you have an ideal setup, none of it will do you any good if there is no signal to pick up at your next location.

Check your carrier coverage map before you embark on your trip. Just because a carrier claims to have coverage doesn't necessarily mean you'll get it or that it'll be a usable signal. These maps do not account for variables such as weather or terrain. You can either search for these maps online or find them on apps such as the Coverage app.

Another good resource for finding cellular is RV Apps.

- **Campendium**

Campendium members have access to coverage maps and signal reviews left by previous campers. You have the option to filter search results by the carrier or whether a park offers free/paid Wi-Fi or not.

- **Allstays**

It also has reviews on cellular coverage for many campgrounds.

So many other apps do the same things; but, Campendium and Allstays do more than just that, as you know from chapter 3.

7

RV PREVENTATIVE MAINTENANCE

It's no secret that a life of adventure in recreational
vehicles is quickly gaining popularity. From Baby
Boomers to Millennials, folks all over America are taking
a deep plunge into road escapades. A curious question remains
for those yet to dive into this lifestyle; How much maintenance
does an RV need? While no straightforward answer truly exists
to that question, we can say that RVs need all the regular maintenance and care that's done on trucks and cars, plus a lot of
extra work. After all, your RV is more than a mere vehicle. It
serves the purposes of an office, living room, kitchen, vacation
getaway, and for many RVers, it is a place they call home.

RV maintenance is just a necessary evil. Without it, one way or
another, your RV will find a way to destroy itself. Again, your
maintenance practices will be influenced by the size and type of
rig you are driving, how much parking and traveling you do,
and your telecommute goals. In this chapter, you will mainly
learn how to do preventative RV maintenance. Preventative
maintenance is regular routine maintenance that helps you
avoid the major problems down the road that are a pain to deal

with. While following all of these steps won't prevent your RV from having any problems, it sure will decrease them.

RV Maintenance and Repairs

RV washing

If you use your RV frequently, then regular washes are your best bet. Washing your RV often helps prevent rust, corrosion, and decay. RVs are more like tiny houses, so washing the dirt and grime off them is more complex than cleaning a regular car. Due to the high amount of water required to clean an RV, most campgrounds rarely let RVers clean their rigs on the grounds. The most practical and effective way to wash your RV would be at home or anywhere you have a steady water supply.

Materials

- Foam Cannon
- Pressure washer
- Mop/soft bristle brush
- Soap
- Ladder
- Bucket of water
- 2-3 Microfiber towels
- Wax

Here are two game-changing tips when washing your RV;

Extra help will come in handy when cleaning your RV, especially if you work in direct sunlight (which you should avoid at all costs). The whole process becomes easy and more efficient when multiple people join hands in the cleaning process. I recommend working as a team with one person rinsing and the other drying. While washing your RV in direct sunlight may be unavoidable, you can try working in the morning or right before sunset when temperatures are much cooler. This way, fewer spots, and streaks will be left in the rig from quick-drying, and you won't get burnt to a crisp from exposure.

You can use a foam cannon and a pressure washer to make the cleaning process faster. You attach the foam cannon to the pressure washer, and it sprays the soapy water all over the RV. Foam cannons, like everything else, can be found on Amazon for 35 dollars. This item is a gamechanger and will save you countless hours cleaning your RV.

Split the RV into these five parts when washing so that you improve efficiency and you don't miss water and soap spots;

- The RV's top section
- The driver's section
- Front of the RV
- Passengers side
- Back of the RV

Always start with the roof. Some roofs are walkable, others not so much. For this reason, rooftops can either be easy or very difficult to clean. Always read the manual before you set foot on the roof. Handle the rooftop carefully, especially around any miscellaneous objects such as antennas, vents, and skylights.

Slipping from this height could be a disaster, so be cautious with that too.

Steps

1. Using a pressure washer, wet a section of the RV. A pressure washer ranging from 1300-1700 PSI should be appropriate. Make sure that you never use the pressure washer's most robust tip (don't attach any angle below 25 degrees). Always keep a safe distance (neither too close nor too long in a single spot) while cleaning. Otherwise, necessary seals and vinyl decals may come off.
2. Spray the side of the RV you are cleaning using a foam cannon. There are many excellent foam cannon soap options available online. Mix the foam cannon soap with water in a ratio of 1:1.
3. Dip your mop/brush into the water bucket and apply it firmly to the RV.
4. Dip your microfiber towel in the water and clean the tires.
5. Rinse everything off using the pressure washer.
6. Repeat until the whole RV is clean.
7. Dry off the RV with microfiber towels. Microfiber towels have up to 200,000 fibers per inch of fabric, so they will efficiently and effectively dry off the RV.
8. Polish off the RV using wax. Waxing your rig may be time-consuming, but doing it at least twice every year adds an extra layer of protection against the elements.

RV waxing is one of the most overlooked parts of RV maintenance. Not only does this wax make your RV look way better, but it leaves a protective layer on the RV. This layer wears away as the months go by, so you should be waxing every few months. Regular waxing ensures your RV is on its A-game, and who doesn't want the best-looking RV in the campground.

Always use special RV wax to avoid oxidation of the fiberglass. You can use paste, liquid, or spray on wax to get the job done. The process takes 1-2.5 hours, depending on the size of your rig. That's because your RV probably has more surface area compared to the average sedan. Test the wax on a small area of the RV first to see how that turns out. Don't forget to have extra caution when applying the wax on decals and seals.

If you are fully committed to high levels of RV cleanliness or if you clean your rig frequently, I recommend looking into water deionizers. Water deionizers enable you to clean your RV without drying it by taking the minerals that cause oxidation out of the water. They cost around $400, but they will save you so much time in the long run because you don't have to dry off your RV anymore.

Waterless wash

Cleaning your RV the traditional way takes a tremendous amount of work and time. But you'd be intrigued to learn that there is a product called Wash Wax All that encapsulates the dirt on your RV so that you can clean it without water while waxing it simultaneously. Wash Wax All has polymers that give your RV a glossy sheen even if you don't polish after washing. It is a high-performance product that is very simple to use. Besides, with Wash Wax All, you will need neither a hose nor a pressure washer. For this reason, you won't have to worry if you are in an area where water is restricted, and you don't need lots of space either.

Wash Wax All is an exceptional 5-star product on Amazon with over 2,000 reviews. If that doesn't make you a believer in WWA, I don't know what will.

Materials

- Microfiber Mop
- Wash Wax All
- Spray Bottle
- Ladder (to get to the top of the RV)

Steps

1. Mix the Wash Wax All with water in the spray bottle in a ratio of 1:1. Feel free to make adjustments depending on how strong you want the mixture to be.
2. Using the spray bottle, wet one side of the microfiber mop with the Wash Wax All mixture and start scrubbing the RV. The mophead should be moist but not wet. Let the mixture sit on the RV for about 1 minute so that all the dirt gets encapsulated. Always use a quality microfiber mophead because without it, the Wash Wax All may not work efficiently.
3. Go back over the side you cleaned using the dry side of the mophead. The Wash Wax All will clean the RV and act as a wax that protects it from the elements.
4. Repeat the process until the RV is clean

This method takes anywhere between 45 minutes- 1.5 hours.

Tires

Distribution of weight

When it comes to weight and handling, driving an RV feels more like a truck. Fifth-wheel trailers, travel trailers, and motorhomes can all be quite hefty. The wide and heavy load makes them susceptible to harsh weather and high winds. For this reason, RV weight distribution, especially around the tires, is crucial.

Sadly, most RVers neglect their tires. For example, when did you last checked the tire pressure. If you own a motorhome, when did you check the inner duals? Better yet, when was the last time you got your rig weighed? Be prepared for sky-high repair costs and unexpected downtimes if you have either inflated tires or an overweight RV because both are unsafe. Most RVers neglect their tires because they don't understand the requirements for proper maintenance.

You'd be intrigued to learn that a study done by Recreation Vehicle Safety Education Foundation reported that more than 25% of RVers overloaded the maximum tire capacity of their rigs. Based on manufacturer specifications, the RVs were over-loaded with more than 900 extra pounds. Another survey done by Firestone showed that out of every 5 RVs, at least 4 had an inflated tire. 1/3 of all the inflated tires were dangerous and could fail at any moment. If that is not bad enough, the extra weight weighed down 40% of all rear tires. All these make sense because RVers are obsessed with filling every nook and cranny of all available space. Today, my goal is to ensure that you don't become another statistic in either overloaded RVs or under-inflated tires.

All tires have a maximum weight capacity for safety reasons. The load shouldn't go past the maximum cargo capacity recom-mended by the manufacturer. Most, if not all manufacturers, come up with weight ratings based on the chain's weakest link. The RV itself, the suspension system, axles, tires, and brakes all have a weak link, and in most cases, the tires are the weakest link.

The weight distribution throughout the RV should be uniform so that no single tire bears most of the load. If you are concerned about your RV's weight distribution, find a vehicle scale and weigh each tire separately to check the load distribution on each tire. Finding a scale shouldn't be a challenge. Just look up truck scales near me on google maps, and a million options will pop up.

The permissible tire load depends on the specific load range and size of a tire. If you want to increase your load capacity, you can change to a tire with a higher load rate but always keep the gross axle weight in mind.

Tire Pressure

Never drive your RV with a tire pressure less than that recommended for the load. If the tire pressure is too little, the sidewalls might flex too much and overheat. Underinflated tires have increased friction which makes them susceptible to overheating and tire blowouts. If the pressure is too much, the traction reduces together with the stopping distance. Overinflated tires are prone to punctures, cuts, and breaks.

Your tires' performance is dependent on the correct PSI (pounds per square inch). Finding a suitable PSI doesn't have to be a challenging task. There are multiple ways to figure out the correct tire pressure and specifications. One method is to find the manufactures' data plates that are usually available for all RVs. The data plates will give correct PSI recommendations depending on the RV's maximum weight load.

Take into account that the scale will recommend the PSI at the maximum weight capacity the RV can handle. So if you load your RV lightly, you will be overinflated if you use the plate's recommendation. To make sure you have the correct tire pressure, you need to get a tire pressure gauge. Gauges cost $5-10 and are worth every penny. Tire gauges allow you to measure the PSI (Pound Per Square Inch) of a tire. Before every trip, you need to check your tires pressure with the gauge.

If you don't maintain the correct tire pressure, the tires may suffer from excess heat build-up, poor handling, and fast tread wear. A tire may lose up to two pounds of air pressure every month. You should therefore check your tire pressure regularly to make necessary adjustments and improvements that are required. Two tires that look the same might have a very different pressure. That's why an accurate pressure gauge is a necessity for your RV. Try to avoid checking the pressure when tires are still hot; you will get a higher pressure reading.

Age and types of Tires

Old age is tough on anyone, and tires are no exception. Most drivers usually replace tires when the treads wear out, but tire life is more than just tread wear. RVs spend a fair amount of their life parked and exposed to damaging UV rays. Sun rays accelerate tire aging, especially on the sidewalls. When the RV is parked on concrete or asphalt, the lubricants in the treads slowly wither away over time.

Long hours of parking will also flat spot and harden your rig's tires. As you can see, parking your RV long-term isn't a good idea. I typically try not to let my RV sit for more than three months without driving it.

Most RV tires have an efficient working life of about five years. However, you can double that period to 10 years with proper maintenance and protection from certain factors such as exposure to UV, rough weather, poor storage, speed, and low inflation.

I would recommend that you get an inspection done on your tires annually after the first five years.

Fortunately, the Department of Transportation designed a method that all RV drivers can use to determine how old a tire is. The uniform tire identification code developed by DOT quickly identifies the manufacture date of the tires. It's worth noting that a tire on a new vehicle may be much older than you think. Maybe the tires had been sitting in the warehouse for a long time before they got installed.

The DOT number is usually located on the inside sidewall of the tire near the rim.

Check the last four digits of the DOT number to understand when a tire was manufactured. The first two numbers of the last four digits will tell you the week the tires were manufactured. The last two numbers show the year the tires were manufactured. For example, if the last four digits of a DOT read 0821, the tires were manufactured in the 8th week of 2021.

Tire covers

Tire covers are vital. They protect your RV tires from elements such as UV exposure, snow, rain, and wind which impact their lifespan. Covering your tires when they are not in use significantly increases their durability.

Tire covers cost approximately $20-50 dollars and are well worth it in the long run.

Tire maintenance

The most important aspect of proper tire care and maintenance is cleanliness. Dirt and oil on the road suck the life out of your tires when you don't maintain them. The soil acts as a sponge that holds the contaminants while the oils degenerate the rubber. If the tires are dry and clean, the natural lubricants that protect them won't erode near as quickly.

You can wash your tires with soap and water occasionally, but don't go beyond that. Excessive washing will eliminate antioxidants and anti-ozone found on the sidewalls because they are meant to protect the tires. I recommend using tire dressing once every few months to protect your tires. Tire dressing cost around 15 dollars and can easily be found on Amazon or any local maintenance and repair shop.

Be careful and avoid tire dressing that contains alcohol, silicone, or petroleum products. These three ingredients can fasten the aging process by causing your tire to crack. As long as your tire dressing doesn't have these harsh chemicals, it should be protected from harmful UV rays.

Leveling out your RV

If you are a regular RVer you've encountered your fair share of unlevelled terrain in RV campsites; if you haven't, trust me, you will soon. Walking, working, or simply sleeping in a sloped RV can be a real nuisance. A slanting position is also not very good for your RV's condition.

Leveling Blocks

Fortunately, leveling blocks, also known as stabilizer pads, jack pads, or stacker blocks, can help in sloping sites or soft grounds. Leveling blocks are an excellent and cheap way to stabilize and control your rig. Leveling blocks are normally made of plastic, but some people use wood too. Place them under the wheels of your rig and then drive up onto them. This will instantly stabilize and even out your rig.

RV Wheel Chocks

A great foundation to build on should be every camper's priority. And if your camper isn't a tent, then chances are it drives on a set of wheels. The stationary base of your RV is a must for comfort and peace of mind.

An unstable vehicle is everybody's nightmare; no one wants to stay inside a rig they can't trust. Sometimes brakes may not always be enough to keep the rig from swaying. This is where wheel chocks come in.

RV wheel chocks are little wedges that keep your RV from moving and swaying while parked. They are the perfect equipment to give your rig the security it needs, especially in uneven terrain. Wheel chocks are an absolute must-have for every type of RV, especially travel trailers and fifth-wheels. Always place the chocks immediately before you unpack at the campsite because removing gear and setting up camp may cause the rig to move.

There are three types of Chocks;

I. Plastic

They are the cheapest, lightest, and most available chocks on the market. Plastic wheel chocks are an excellent choice and will get the job done, but they can be a little risky when used on heavier rigs. These cost anywhere from $5-15 per pair and will work just fine 99% of the time, especially on tandem and single axle trailers.

II. Rubber chocks

These are an upgrade from plastic chocks. They offer more friction and aren't limited by wheel size because they have more height. Rubber chocks are the most reliable option if you are committed to your rig steady. They are beasts and can last for years, even when faced with harsh weather conditions. Rubber chocks are also way easier to use and remove compared to plastic chocks. They are a few more dollars, but you can't go wrong with them. I recommend using rubber over plastic chocks any day.

III. X Chocks

Unlike the other chocks, X Chocks are designed to fit in between two sets of tires. The X-chock is fitted between the tires, tightened, and expanded, creating pressure against the tires. X chocks will not prevent your trailer from moving down a slope, so you will still need either plastic or rubber chocks for your rig. They are really just meant to limit the movement of the trailer or fifth-wheel while you are walking around inside. These cost anywhere from 60- 100 dollars, and I only recommend them if your rig is noticeably unstable.

So how many chocks do you need?

Weight and incline grade determine how many wheel chocks you need for your RV. Smaller RVs may only need one or two pairs, but larger motorhomes may require four pairs of wheel chocks. I recommend using two-wheel chocks per tire; I'd rather be safe than sorry.

Which one?

Use leveling blocks if you have a motorhome and chocks if you have a trailer.

Jacks

As you know, not every campsite is going to be concrete and well-leveled for your RV or trailer setup. This is why most large RVs come with built-in jacks. An RV stabilizer jack is a metal arm that's installed into your RV's frame and designed to extend from the frame of the RV onto the ground. Jacks stabilize your RV and prevent it from moving while you walk around in the rig.

Jacks come in multiple variations (lengths, strengths, and styles) and can be electric or manual. Because every RV is unique, there is no a "one-size-fits-all" jack. This means that you must narrow down your choices and get what works for your rig.

Jacks will;

- Keep your RV leveled
- Protect your tires
- Stabilize your rig

You also might need a jack if you are driving smaller rigs like class Cs or travel trailers. The jack and the rig need to be compatible. Always consult with your RV dealer because the wrong jack could damage your RV.

Awning Maintenance

There's nothing better than an RV awning to block the sun and provide some shade on a hot summer day, but like anything, they require maintenance. There's a lot to watch out for with awnings, from mildew issues to forgetting to close them during your travels. They are notorious problem makers if not properly cared for. Fortunately, these problems can be dealt with easily. Awnings are generally easier to clean because they rarely get dirty unless you find yourself in a dusty area. Whether manual or electric, they will both require the same level of maintenance.

Awnings and Elements

If you find yourself in a storm, try to angle one corner of the awning downwards. This way, water won't build up or pool at the center; instead, it will run off quickly. Water is heavy and can cause rips and tears to the awning fabric. Ensure the awning is completely dry before rolling it up or putting it away because moisture provides a suitable environment for mildew growth, deterioration, and staining. Try not to leave awnings out in high winds or extreme weather. RV awnings are made of simple fabrics that are not designed to withstand strong winds. Any winds over 20 mph can easily damage them.

Cleaning your Awning

Proper cleaning of your awning will prolong its functional years. We all hate dirty awnings, especially if the smell of mildew starts to creep in.

Materials

- Awning cleaner/ cleaning solution
- Spray Bottle Hose/ Pressure washer
- Soft bristle brush/ Mop

Steps

1. Clear any dirt, leaves, and debris from the awning. Lower it down as far as possible and spray both sides with the cleaning solution. You can use either an awning cleaner or a homemade solution such as dish soap and water.
2. Roll up the awning so that the solution can soak. Let it sit for 30 minutes to an hour.
3. Use a brush or mop to wipe both sides of the fabric. Put some elbow grease into it but don't be too aggressive.
4. Rinse the awning thoroughly with a hose or pressure washer. Make sure all traces of the cleaning solution are removed so that the fabric isn't damaged.
5. Let the awning dry out, and then roll it up for storage.

Rooftop

Routine roof maintenance can go a long way in protecting your rig from leaks and rotting. If you neglect your roof, your rig will be rendered inoperable by water damage and mold. What's worse, most rooftop issues aren't covered by insurance or warranties. If damage occurs on the roof, you're on your own. You should check your roof for cracks, rips, tears, and caulking separations periodically. Knowing how to care for your RV's roof will help you stay one step ahead in preventing expensive repairs and harmful leaks.

Rooftop Types

Many people wonder what RV roofs are made of. Understanding the kind of roof your rig has is critical in the maintenance method you use.

There are four main types of roofs;

I. Rubber EPDM

EPDM (Ethylene Propylene Diene Monomer) is the most common type of rubber roof. It is a highly durable type of synthetic rubber roofing membrane. Additionally, EPDM is easy to install and cheap to purchase. The membranes in EPDM roofs are resistant to wind, hail, UV radiation, thermal shock, and extreme temperatures. The material used in EPDM has an average life span of 25-30 years. It is resistant to leaks, doesn't scratch, and can withstand harsh elements. On the flip side, it comes in darker colors that absorbs lots of heat, raising the temperatures inside the RV.

II. Rubber TPO

TPO (Thermoplastic Polyolefin) is a roofing membrane made of a single layer of synthetic fiber. It is a cost-effective option which makes it a common choice among RVers. TPO is usually white, which helps the rubber reflect off harmful UV rays. It is slightly more expensive than EPDM and will last around 15-20 years. TPO can be maintained the same way as EPDM roofs because they are very similar.

A downside to rubber roofs is that they are more susceptible to damage from harsh weather and low-hanging limbs. For this reason, frequent cleaning (every 3-4) months will increase their durability. Avoid using any form of petroleum-based products for cleaning. They will do irreversible damage to these roofs.

TPO is the way to go if you are interested in efficiency and aesthetics, but you can choose EPDM if you long for longevity and durability.

III. Fiberglass

A fiberglass roof is a composite laminate material formed by combining polyester and delicate strands of fiberglass. It comes in the form of panels and sheets. A fiberglass roof will protect your RV better because it has no welds, seams, and joints that can cause leakages. Fiberglass roofs are a favorite among RVers because they are customizable and lightweight. Fiberglass roofs can last up to 30 years and are resistant to rust, fire, and decay. They are more expensive but easy to care for and maintain. Unlike TPO, fiberglass isn't very good at handling heat from the sun. When exposed to extreme heat for too long, they can experience thermal splits, which are expensive to fix. Always add a wax application after cleaning to protect it from the elements.

IV. Aluminum

This type of roof consists of silver-white metal made from sheets of aluminum. They do great in acid-rain environments and coastal climates because they are resistant to saltwater corrosion. Aluminum roofs are incredibly durable, and for that reason, they are the most expensive roof option available.

Like fiberglass roofs, aluminum requires slightly less maintenance than rubber roofs. The best way to repair structural damage on aluminum roofs is Eterna bond seam tape. This tape is extremely sturdy and should always be in your toolkit if you have an aluminum roof. These roofs can last up to 50 years if cared for properly, but this doesn't mean they will always look great.

Roof Maintenance

Consider doing preventative roof maintenance every 3 to 4 months. Many people recommend specialized roof cleaning products, but good old-fashioned soap and water will always get the job done.

Sealing

If you want to keep your maintenance costs low, you must learn how to repair roof punctures yourself. No matter what type of roof you have, it's essential to seal it. Experts recommend fresh seal application even when there aren't major RV issues. Additionally, recoating and resealing things like vents and air conditioners at least once a year can really improve your rig's roof.

Water is the #1 cause of RV damage, so you will need to use sealants around anything that could pose a potential problem. Sealing doesn't just stop at the roof; you will need to seal things like windows, showers, and doors as well. Routine sealing of your RV is crucial.

Always add an RV roof tape/roof patch to your toolkit, just in case. For example, a low branch may tear your roof while on the road, and you will be grateful you carried some roof tape. Roof tape is easy to use, and it doesn't peel away easily, which means the fix can last for years.

Materials

- Roof sealant
- Lap sealant
- Sealant remover spray
- Chalk remover tool
- Paper towels/Rags

Some of the top sealant brands for your roof include;

- Dicor Roof Sealant
- Eternabond

Top Brands for the rest of your RV

- Proflex
- Dicor Lap Sealant

How to seal Your RV

Steps

1. Spray the open or cracked area with caulk remover spray and clean it using your rag. My favorite brand of sealant remover spray is Goo Gone spray instead of the more popular brand Coleman Camping Fuel. Goo Gone spray is more efficient and less harsh on surfaces than Camping Fuel.
2. If there is any old/useless sealant in the cracked area, remove it with a caulk remover. You can always find a good caulk remover on Amazon for $5-10.
3. Go over the damaged area with the sealant and be careful not to put too much. Using a caulking gun will improve the efficiency and ease of the application process. You can get one on Amazon for $15.

Check your seals for cracks every few months to avoid huge expenses later on.

RV roof covers

If you are not storing your RV indoors – which is expensive but better— it would be a good idea to purchase a roof cover. Not only are they UV resistant, but they are also waterproof. They will increase the lifespan of your roof by protecting it from the harsh elements. Any rig that is left sitting can suffer severe harm from hail, rain, and UV rays. The better the roof cover fits, the better it protects the RV. There are tons of covers out there, so it shouldn't be too hard to find one that fits.

While a good cover ensures that moisture evaporates from the roof, mildew may still grow under it. That's because the covering doesn't allow light to penetrate through. This is why I recommend not storing your RV for too long.

You can keep it on during the storage season, but don't keep it on the roof longer than necessary if you want to avoid mildew. Alternatively, you can purchase a full RV cover. A complete RV cover protects the roof and the rest of the rig. They are weather-resistant and can extend the lifespan of your RV's exterior coat and paint.

Lubrication

Most RVs come with modern home conveniences and trust me, they don't run themselves. Without a shadow of a doubt, some part of the RV will fail at some point. Lubricating the RV is the most straightforward preventative maintenance job an RV owner can do, but it's usually overlooked or forgotten. Spending just 15 minutes of your time lubricating your RV from time to time can increase its lifespan significantly.

All you need is;

- RV Lubricant
- Microfiber towel

Recommended lube Brands

- RV care
- Camco
- Thetford

Things that need lube;

RV Slideouts

Slideouts are great and add lots of extra space to your floorplan. When they aren't maintained well, slideouts can freeze, either in the in or out position. Imagine if the slideout malfunctions and leaves you stranded on moving day; what a bummer. You need an efficient slideout care routine if you want to avoid a myriad of complex issues.

Start by cleaning the slideouts with a towel before lubricating them. This prevents the build-up of dirt and grime that sticks to the lubricant when it's applied.

Other things that need lubricate include;

- Entry door
- Window tracks
- Awning hardware
- Lock cylinders
- Stabilizer Jacks

Exercise the moving parts as you are lubricating to get the maximum benefit of the lubricant.

RV Water

Side note- Before you do anything with the tanks, make sure you have a high-quality food-grade water hose.

The environment inside your water tanks creates the perfect environment for the growth of bacteria and mold, especially during warmer months. Just imagine what can grow in a moist tank when the tank is just sitting around for months. I'd rather not think about it. This is why you should clean your tanks frequently. If not frequently, at least try and clean it before you store the RV for winter.

Holding tanks

I. Fresh-water tank

Water that comes out of your taps gets stored in the freshwater tank. Typically, a city water connection pumps the water into the tank via a portable hose. Always make sure you have a water filter at the end of your portable hose to be on the safe side.

II.Gray water Tank

The dirty water from your RV shower and the kitchen sink is held in your grey water tank. Some vintage RVs and campers may lack the gray water tank.

III. Blackwater tanks

Water from the toilet is held in the black water tank. The black water tank tends to scare new RVers, but they are manageable when treated with care.

Toilet Paper

Please don't use regular toilet paper in RVs because they don't dissolve in water. Use toilet paper specifically designed for RVs because it dissolves, making it safer for the black water tank. Not using the right toilet paper is one of the most common reasons for plumbing issues.

Some good options include;

- Scott Rapid dissolving toilet paper
- Camco RV bathroom toilet tissue
- Angel Soft toilet Paper

Emptying tanks

While RVing may create wonderful memories, some parts of it aren't very pretty. It's unglamorous to empty and clean your tanks, but it is necessary. You must learn to care for your tanks properly; otherwise, things can get ugly. Several factors will affect the frequency at which you empty the tanks. If you are traveling with family, you may need to empty your tanks every other day; if it is just you and your spouse, once a week may be enough. A general rule of thumb is to wait until your tanks are about two-thirds full before emptying them. Most RVs have an onboard sensor system that you can use to check the levels of each individual tank.

You can use chemicals that are designed to control odor for both grey and black water systems.

Always flush the systems regularly and with enough water.

If you don't do proper wastewater maintenance, you will have to deal with clogging issues, excess build-up, and odor.

Materials

- Gloves
- Sewer hose

Steps

1. Locate the holding tank's outlet and find the valves on your RV's outer section (typically marked and found at the back of the rig).
2. Make sure the cap that covers the holding tank outlets has been removed. Connect the holding tank to the blackwater sewer hose. Take the other end of the hose and put it in the dump hole, at least 4-5 inches deep. Fasten the hose well on both ends before you pull the valves. Invest in a good quality sewer hose; cheap ones often get pinholes causing sprays out.
3. Pull the black water valve first and let the tank drain completely. The draining should take anywhere from 1-5 minutes, and you should hear the draining sounds. Always start with the black water tank so the gray tank water can flush out anything left in the sewer line.
4. When you no longer hear any of the liquid coming through the hose, you can close the valve.
5. Empty the gray water tank and close the valve. Some RVers leave the valve for the gray tank open at all times (when they are hooked up to the sewer, however, I recommend closing your valves).
6. Flush a Bio enzyme treatment into the black water tank after emptying them. Enzyme treatments use proteins to break down waste and prevent residue from forming inside the tank. Treatments come in several forms, including powders, drop-in packets, and liquids.

You can find millions of bio enzymes designed for RV use on Amazon. I also recommend dropping them in your sink or shower occasionally to clean out the gray water tank.

Draining your freshwater tank is simple. Just release the drain valve on the bottom; you don't need to dispose of the freshwater, unlike like the black and gray water.

Propane Tanks

Propane tanks are like the nerve center of every RV. They provide your furnace, stove, heating systems, and fridge with power. Without them, you wouldn't have hot water, a functioning heating system, or a working fridge. There are two main types of propane tanks;

I. ASME Tanks

They are also known as horizontal propane tanks because of how they are placed in the RV. Most motorhomes use ASME tanks. These tanks are mounted directly to the frame of the RV, which means they are not removable. ASME tank sizes can vary significantly from one motorhome to another. A smaller class C motorhome may have a single 20-pound ASME tank, while a large class A motorhome may come with a tank holding over 100 pounds of propane.

II. DOT Cylinders

DOT cylinders are often used on truck campers, travel trailers, fifth wheels, and smaller motorhomes. These vessels are smaller than ASME tanks and are very portable. DOT cylinders are mounted on either the tongue or bumper of the RV. They can also be stored in one of the RV's exterior compartments.

Most RVers use RV propane tank covers to shield their tanks from extreme weather conditions and road grime. Many tank covers are made of polypropylene and have a wide range of colors and sizes to choose from. They are very convenient and easy to remove.

Tank Gauges

On one of my camping trips on a late fall evening, I woke up cold and almost froze to death in my sleep. Do you know why? Well, my furnace stopped because I had run out of propane. I was unable to monitor my propane levels and was left without gas when I needed it the most. Don't let this happen to you. A fuel gauge is one of the easiest and most reliable ways of measuring how much propane is left in the tank. With the tank gauge, you will know how much propane is left in the tank so that you don't run out of it unknowingly and put yourself in difficult situations.

ASME tanks typically have an RV propane tank gauge pre-installed. However, DOT cylinder owners will have to purchase one. You can find meters on Amazon or at local stores. They cost around $15 per gauge and are a necessity if you plan on using propane. Monitoring your propane levels on a rig must be done. Never sit around guessing how much propane you have left.

Filling your tank

You can fill up your propane tank in multiple places, such as gas stations, truck stations, and RV parks. Typically most RV sites will have propane refill stations. Sites that don't have them will direct you to nearby dealers.

Don't pump your propane if you are inexperienced. The employees will help you if you don't know how to do it.

Since ASME tanks are usually mounted directly on a motorhome's frame, you will have to drive your RV to the station or propane dealer to get a refill. On the contrary, DOT cylinders can be removed easily and taken to the dealer for a refill because they are portable.

8

THE RV ELECTRICAL SYSTEM

The RV electrical system, it's either your best friend or worst enemy. Electricity is the only thing that separates an RV from traditional camping. As long as it's intact, you're able to enjoy the comforts of a residential home. However, when it's not working, you feel like your back in the stone age - no lights, no fridge, no smartphone = no Facebook and Instagram. The electrical system allows you to utilize overhead lighting, vent fans, refrigerators, microwaves, and many other things.

While having access to all these things on the road is incredible, you must understand how an RV electrical system works. Basic knowledge of RV power sources and wiring will help you make informed decisions while you are on the road. More so, you'll understand where to draw power from and troubleshoot if the RV electrical system isn't working right.

In this chapter, you will learn all the basics of an RV's electrical system. I do realize that most RVers aren't engineers, and neither am I. Some guides describe an RV electrical system in such a complex way that I was left feeling like I needed a NASA engineer to assist me with my rig's setup. Therefore, I will try to simplify the process as much as possible. Your RV, just like a regular "sticks and bricks" home, is dependent on a 120 and 12 volt power system. These two systems are Direct Current (DC) and Alternating Current (AC).

Direct Current

DC is a 12-volt system that's powered by a battery or multiple batteries in the RV. Direct current is routinely used on small-ticket items like lights, water pumps, water heaters, fans, carbon monoxide detectors, TV, and the radio. This system runs the RV when you are not plugged into an external power source. The DC system should have a cumulative total of 12 volts. One 12-volt battery can provide enough DC to run an RV's essential appliances.

Alternating Current

AC is a 120- volt system powered by an external AC power source such as shore power or a generator. The AC system generates way more power compared to the Direct Current system. Big appliances like the air conditioning, microwave, and power outlets, run off this power system.

Think of the two systems this way;

- AC power source allows you to enjoy all of the luxuries of an RV.
- DC power enables you to use the essentials like lights and a water pump for a few days.

These two RV electrical systems work concurrently. For example, when AC power is coming from the RV, it charges up the batteries for a DC system with the help of a converter. Alternatively, an inverter turns DC power into AC.

Converter

Basically, a converter takes higher voltage electricity and converts it down to a lower voltage. Most RVs will take 120 volt AC power and convert it down to 12 volt DC power. Basically, when you are plugged into shore power, the converter allows you to charge your batteries back up.

Inverter

Inverters basically do the opposite of converters. In a nutshell, they allow you to use 120 volt AC power when you are not plugged into shore power or running off a generator. Most RVs are built with a converter; however, not all of them come with an inverter.

There are two types of inverters:

I. Modified Sine

The main feature of a modified sine converter is a waveform. It is suitable for running resistive loads like appliances and lines. They're a cost-effective and reliable choice, but they reduce the efficiency of the equipment in use. Another drawback is that more power is drawn from the inverter by motors because of the low efficiency. For example, a refrigerator working on a sine wave inverter will be less efficient compared to when it is working on another type of inverter. You are likely to hear some noise from appliances running on these types of inverters too. Please do not get one of these for your RV.

II. Pure Sine

A pure sine wave inverter is the best choice for powering electronic equipment in your RV. It produces a replica of AC power to keep appliances running smoothly. Pure sines are a costly option, but they support more devices and run them smoothly like at home. Get a pure sine inverter if you want to use AC power while you are still unplugged.

Power Sources

Many people are intrigued by RVs. They wonder how RVers get access to essential utilities while they are on the road. How do they cook, bathe, or even run an AC?

But what happens when you are far away from civilization, at a random grassland somewhere in Montana?

Well, RVs can operate from multiple power sources such as

- propane tanks
- batteries
- generators
- solar panels
- inverters
- shore power

Let's explore these power sources;

Shore Power

Shore power is a phrase commonly used to refer to marine vessels plugged into a primary grid electrical system when they are docked at a marina. It also refers to RVs plugged into an electrical grid, coming from a campground pedestal or another outlet. A power cord connects the pedestal to the RV, which converts the energy to electricity used inside the rig. Shore power runs the AC system and is measured in amps.

Amps are the base unit of electrical current, and RVs either run on 30 amps or 50 amps, depending on the size. Typically, if you have one AC unit, the voltage is 30 amp, and if you have two, the voltage is 50 amp.

30 amp

Smaller RVs like travel trailers and class C's are usually powered by 30 amp volts. A 30-amp RV has one 30-amp circuit breaker, and everything runs off of it. A 30 amp plugs use three prongs to connect to the power source. It is the most common type of shore power, but it can barely run appliances like an air conditioner and a microwave at the same time. Pretty much all campsites have 30-amp shore power.

50 amp

Larger RVs, especially those that are equipped with two air conditioners, run on 50 amps. Such RVs utilize up to 3 times more power compared to 30-amp RVs. One significant distinction is that 50-amp plugs use four prongs to connect, with two of them giving 50 amps of power each. The RV can therefore use up to 100 amps at a time. A 50-amp RV can power multiple appliances such as two air conditioners, a microwave, a washer or dryer, and a TV simultaneously with no risk of tripping the breaker. Unlike 30 amp power, 50 amp power is not always guaranteed at every campsite.

Adapter

The availability of feature-rich comforts is what makes RVing appealing. For those comforts to be available, you must plug electronics and appliances into a power source. Most RVers know that electrical connections aren't always straightforward. You may only have a 50-amp plug when the campsite only has 30-amp outlets and vice versa.

You absolutely need an adapter no matter where you're camping. Fortunately, adapters allow you to manipulate the physical shape of the campsite outlet to fit the needs of your RV.

Adapters are great, but they do not alter the power output. If you plug a 50 amp RV into a 30 amp pedestal, you will maximize at 30 amps because that's all the power it can supply. If you plug a 30 amp RV into a 50 amp pedestal, the adapter will limit you to a 30 amp max capacity.

All RVers should travel with an adapter, even if they are on a 30-amp rig. This way, you can always be prepared if a campsite doesn't have your rig's exact power capacity. The most important thing you need to know is how many amps you are using. Drawing too much power from the shore line or more power than your rig is rated for can be dangerous.

- 50 amp- you can use up to 100 amps at a time
- 30 amp- you are limited to 30 amps

While I am not an electrician by any stretch of the imagination, I will help you with an am chart showing the average amperage drawn out by regular accessories found in RVs. This basic guide will help you understand how many amps your equipment is using at any given time.

AMPS per object;

- Lights (per bulb) .5-1.5 amps
- Converter 1-8 amps
- Water heater 8-13 amps
- AC 12-15 amps per unit
- Fan 3-5 amps
- Space heater 8-13 amps
- Refrigerator 2-4 amps
- Blender 5-6 amps
- Microwave 12-15 amps
- Toaster 8-10 amps
- Coffee maker 5-8 amps
- Hairdryer 7-13 amps
- Curling iron .5-.7 amps
- Iron 8-10 amps
- Washer/ dryer 14-16 amps
- TV 1.5-4 amps
- Chargers .5-1.5 amps

Generators

If you have an RV generator, you can enjoy the comforts of a home while you are camping off-grid or unplugged. Some RVs come with built-in generators, while others have portable ones.

Built in Generator

Built-in generators are most commonly associated with large fifth wheels and motorhomes. They are engine-driven and use fuel to generate AC power. These generators are hardwired, which means that when they are pumped up, it automatically fires up the rig. Most built-in generators are easy to use and can be kicked off with the push of a button. Built-in generators commonly run on 2500-7000 watts. They are easy to fuel, and you won't experience power interruptions during storms.

Portable Generator

Portable generators are more common in smaller rigs such as campers and travel trailers. Their low cost and luxury of mobility makes them very common amongst RVers. They run on approximately 2000-4000 watts and use gasoline as fuel. Portable generators have smaller fuel tanks and require frequent fueling compared to built-in generators.

Beware, portable generators have a high theft risk so make sure to lock them up. Most portable generators do not have adequate protection from rain and should not be exposed to water or harsh elements.

Generators come in many different sizes, but most small ones do not provide near as much energy as shoreline power. Generators are rated in watts, so the more watts a generator has, the more power it provides. However, many people desire peace of nature when RVing, yet generators are loud, large, heavy, and require multiple refills. For this reason, generators may not be ideal for every traveler.

Types of Generators

The main distinction between different types of RV generators lies in the type of fuel source used. Most generators are powered by either gas or diesel, while others use liquid propane.

Propane Genorators

Propane generators are the least expensive generator because it runs on propane which is the cheapest fuel. These types of generators use vent pipes and mufflers to release emissions. Just like other generators, propane generators have an alternating element to convert AC to DC. Although most propane generators produce less noise, you're still going to hear it.

Pros

- Least expensive generator
- Easily accessible
- Propane has a long shelf life
- They emit low amounts of harmful substances for a cleaner environment

Cons

- Not very powerful
- Have to refill propane often
- Propane can be dangerous when it gets spilled

If you don't need too much power a propane generator might be for you.

Gasoline

This type of generator runs on, you guessed it, gas. Gasoline generators are popular because gasoline is readily available. Gas is available in small sizes, which is ideal for portability. Be careful because, as you know, gas is highly flammable. These generators are inexpensive and easily accessible.

Pros

- Very easy and cost-effective to refill
- Have more power than propane-powered generators
- You can power more appliances at a given time

Cons

- Shorter life span
- Highly flammable

A gas-powered generator is a good choice if you have a mid-sized RV that uses a moderate amount of power.

Diesel

Diesel generators are the most powerful type of RV generator. They use diesel as fuel and come in different sizes, designs, and models. These devices automatically transfer power from a grid to the generator during a power surge. They provide a clean power option, but they are not as clean as their propane and gas counterparts.

Pros

- Most powerful of the generator types
- Safer than gasoline-powered generators
- Most reliable and rugged
- Easy to access fuel
- Relatively low maintenance

Cons

- Most expensive generator
- They emit hazardous exhaust fumes

If you have a large RV that runs on diesel, this is a great option.

The two most trusted brands of generators are ;

- Honda
- Yamaha

Factors to Consider When Choosing an RV Generator

If you plan to camp in areas without electricity, having a portable generator comes in handy. Over the years, generators have evolved tenfold in performance and design. With state-of-the-art technology improvements, RV generators have become much easier to use.

Some of the factors to consider include:

Size

When it comes to picking the size of your RV generator, the most important aspect is the electrical output. In general, portable generators can use anywhere from 3,000-7,000 watts of power. While built-in generators range from 8,000-12,000 watts. Just like each object runs off a certain amount of amps, the same things apply to watts.

There are two types of watts;

- Running watts- how many watts it takes to run the appliance
- Starting Watts- additional watts needed for 2-3 seconds while starting the appliance

This guide will show you how many watts each object needs;

Running WattsWatts

- Light Bulb 60 W
- Fan 200 W
- Rooftop AC 1200 W
- Refrigerator 700 W
- Water heater 1440 W
- Blow Dryer 1250 W
- Curling Iron 850 W
- Washer/Dryer 1150 W
- Vacum 1100 W
- Microwave 600 W
- Coffee Maker 1000 W
- Dishwasher 1500 W
- Toaster 850 W

Additional Starting Watts

- Light Bulb 0
- Fan 400 W
- Rooftop AC 3600 W
- Refrigerator 2200 W
- Water heater 1440 W
- Blow Dryer 1250 W
- Curling Iron 0
- Washer/Dryer 3450 W
- Vacum 0
- Microwave 0
- Coffee Maker 0
- Dishwasher 1500 W
- Toaster 0

To be on the safe side, never go above 80 percent of what the generator can handle. This way, your generator won't suffer the consequences of running at full power. Just like amps, never go over the watt rating, this is dangerous and can cause many problems.

The size of the generator you get really depends on how many appliances you want to run.

Here is another general guide

3000-5000 watts- can run the basic appliances

5,000-8,00 watts- can run most of your appliances

8,000- 12000 watts- can run everything in the RV

All of this information is just a starting point. Everyone's situation is different, so you will need to do your research and figure out how much power your RV needs.

Altitude

Some generators will lose performance when operated at high elevations due to reduced oxygen levels and low atmospheric pressure. The performance drops off don't usually occur until you are 500 feet above sea level. A generator typically experiences a 3.5 percent power decline for every 1,000 feet above an altitude of 500 feet.

A generator is a substantial financial investment. Thus, you need to check the warranty and what's included. The best generator should offer reliability, high performance, longevity, and stability.

Batteries

Batteries work as a power supply when you need it most. They can provide your RV with a source of DC electricity when no external power is available. Batteries are typically a weaker power source that can run smaller appliances like the TV, toaster, light bulbs, etc. They usually struggle with big-ticket items like the air conditioning or heating systems.

Batteries are typically not the main source of power, but they are great for powering your RV between campsites. Most batteries are not a reliable long-term power source and generally last one night before needing to be recharged. In most rigs, your battery charges any time an external power source is connected, such as shore power or a generator. As long as you have a converter.

RV batteries run on amps. You can use a simple formula to figure out how many amps per hour your battery uses. Battery amp hour rating divided by hours used equals amps available per hour.

10- amp hour battery/ 8hours= 12.5 amps per hour

The number of amps per hour depends on how much power you are using. Think of it like gas mileage. If you are flooring it every chance you get and going fast, the gas won't last very long. Now, if you drive conservatively, the gas will last much longer. The same applies to RV batteries, the more power you use at once, the shorter the life span.

It's imperative never to let your batteries die or get too low. A good rule of thumb is; never let the batteries get below 50 percent power. The battery's life expectancy depends on you. The sooner a battery is recharged, the better.

Here are some tips to help you maintain your battery life;

1. Follow routine maintenance and recharge the battery as soon as possible. Sulfation is the leading cause of dead batteries. When the battery gets low, tiny crystals start forming on the plates in a process called sulfation. If this remains for an extended period, the battery life will be reduced.
2. Ensure your 12-volt battery never goes below 12 volts. Typically, a fully charged battery is 12.7 volts, and when it gets below 12 volts can reduce its life span.
3. Hot temperatures kill batteries. If you're in hot areas, ensure you check water levels in battery cells regularly.
4. Adding distilled water and checking electrolyte levels after charging can save lead-acid batteries. Ensure you add mineral-free water because regular tap water can cause sulfation.

Surge Protector

When you pull into your campground site, it's tempting to plug right in and turn everything on. However, you want to keep safety in mind. Surge protectors ensure that the RV shore power is clean and steady before the electricity enters your rig. They act as a guard from power surges, both natural and unnatural.

There are two types of surge protectors for RVs:

Regular surge protector

Regular surge protectors are the cheapest type of protectors and will only shield your electrical system from severe overvoltage conditions. You do not want to go the cheap route here; avoid regular surge protectors.

EMS Surge protector

An EMS (energy management system) is the best RV surge protector you can get. They range anywhere from 200-400 dollars and are well worth the investment.

EMS protectors will protect your RV from many conditions such as:

- Under voltage
- Overvoltage
- Reverse polarity
- Open neutral
- Open ground
- High and low frequency
- VAC voltage

Anytime an EMS surge protector senses one of these problems, it immediately cuts off power to your RV.

If it has three prongs, it's a 30 AMP protector

If it has four prongs, it's a 50 AMP protector

Features and Specifications

Knowing the features to look for and understanding basic specifications can help you pick the best surge protector for your RV.

Joules – This is the maximum amount of energy a surge protector can absorb. It comes into play if there is a power surge or voltage spike in a power grid. Therefore, the higher the Joule rating, the better.

Permanent surge protector

Permanent or hardwired protectors are fixed permanently inside the rig: between the electronics and power pedestal.

Pros

- Easy and fast to set up
- It's in-built in your RV, so no worries about harsh weather conditions
- It cannot be stolen because it is built-in

Cons

- Must get installed

Portable surge protector

A portable surge protector is the one you can plug into a power pedestal.

Pros

- Easy to replace
- No installation needed
- Seamless portability

Cons

- Susceptible to weather
- It can get stolen easily

If you are going to take all this time to set up your RV's electrical system, you might as well invest in a surge protector. Which one? That's up to you.

Solar power

Old solar panels were impractical for most RVers. Back in the day, they were expensive, unreliable, and bulky. Today, they are gaining popularity as environmentally friendly, cheap, reliable, and customizable options. Don't get me wrong, solar power is totally worth the investment, but it has a few downsides too. You will be facing a hefty upfront cost; however, you will have the freedom to access power anywhere. The solar panels convert the sun's cells' energy into electrical current, which your RV can then use for power. The resulting electrical current is fed through wires and turned into a DC power source. Basically solar panels charge up your batteries. Solar power can run small essential appliances such as lights, fans, and your TV.

With solar panels, you are still limited by the amount of energy your battery can provide. Fortunately, you can recharge it over time without having to plug it into an external power source. Solar setups can be costly, ranging from $1500 upwards. You should only invest in solar power if you plan on keeping your RV for an extended period. So, for your first few trips, stay away from solar energy!

CONCLUSION

The joy and anticipation that comes with sitting behind the wheel of your new RV can be overwhelming. There is a lot to look forward to; the dusty roads, wild spaces, national parks, and breathtaking historical sites. Endless adventure lies ahead. The process of buying, preparing, and taking your RV on that first trip doesn't have to be hard. When the beauty and accessibility of the open road beckons for the next adventure, put to use everything you have learned in this book. Take time to create your budget. Make sure you keep up with your RV's maintenance schedule and always inspect to make sure everything works fine. You already know the perks of RVing along open roads with all the comforts of a modern home. If you decide to take a cross-country trip right now, I am confident that you will have the time of your life.

If there is one piece of advice I can leave you with, it's this: the RV lifestyle is worth it!

ABOUT THE AUTHOR

J. W. Warren is an emerging author who has just begun. He just turned 21 and is looking to continue his career in writing, with several books in the making. James just began his career as a Shopify drop-shipper but has since decided to pursue a career as an author. If you enjoyed the content, it would be greatly appreciated if you left a review on Amazon and joined James's Facebook group RV Minds.